Sarah Josepha Hale

1788-1879

Sarah Josepha Hale. Silhouette by Edouart

Used by permission of National Portrait Gallery, Smithsonian
Institution, Washington, D.C. On loan from an anonymous giver.

Sarah Josepha Hale

A New England Pioneer

1788-1879

by
Sherbrooke Rogers

Tompson
&
Rutter
Grantham, New Hampshire

Library of Congress Cataloging in Publication Data

Rogers, Sherbrooke, 1916-
    Sarah Josepha Hale: a New England Pioneer,
    1788-1879.
    Bibliography: p. 131
    Includes index.
    1. Hale, Sarah Josepha Buell, 1788-1879.
    2. Journalists—United States—Biography.
    I. Title.
PN4874.H22R6 1985   070.4′8347′0294 [B]   84-20520
ISBN 0-936988-10-X

Acknowledgments

The quotations from the letters of Matthew Vassar are used by permission of Vassar College. The letters are the property of the College.

The quotation from "Mr. Godey's Lady" by Ralph Nading Hill (*American Heritage*, October 1958) is used by permission of the author.

To Webb with love

Contents

We cannot learn, neither can we teach, by a sort of magic peculiar to ourselves: give us the facilities for education enjoyed by the other sex, and we shall at least be able to try what are the capabilities of women.

Sarah Josepha Hale
Godey's *Lady's Book*
August 1837

Preface

In 1972 when I first began studying the life and times of Sarah Josepha Hale, the question almost invariably asked was "Who is she?" Although her many accomplishments were known by people in her native town of Newport, New Hampshire, few others had ever heard her name, and those few knew her solely as the author of "Mary's Lamb." My purpose in writing Sarah Hale's story has been to secure for this gifted American the honored place in our country's history she so richly deserves.

I also hope my method of presentation will make Sarah Hale come alive in the mind of the reader. This has been difficult because although her professional life as an author, social reformer, and the long-time editor of Godey's *Lady's Book* placed her very much in the public eye, her personal life was an entirely different matter. She believed strongly that autobiographical details should not be published in a magazine she edited. However, and fortunately, she did write facts about her life in the prefaces of her many published books.

I have read, and quoted from, the writings of Sarah Hale, mainly those appearing in the *Ladies' Magazine* and the *Lady's Book*, but also from her books: *Northwood, Manners, The Ladies Wreath, Flora's Interpreter, Woman's Record*, and her poems: "Address to the Sugar River," "Mary's Lamb," and "Love: On Woman's Destiny." Other quotation sources are indicated by asterisks in the bibliography.

I would like to express my appreciation and thanks to Jean

Galloway and her staff at Richards Free Library, Newport, and to acknowledge others who aided and encouraged me in my writing; Evan Hill, Susan Menke, Edward DeCourcy, Barbara Yeomans, and a special friend, Alma Ohler.

1 Early Years

The plaintive whistle of a train passing through Newport, New Hampshire, would not be heard until almost a century later, and stage coach service was thirty-five years in the future when Sarah's parents, Gordon and Martha Whittlesey Buell, arrived in town after a long, dusty, and tedious journey by wagon from Saybrook, Connecticut, early in the summer of 1783. Newport was little more than a raw settlement with a general store, saw and grist mills, a Congregational and a Baptist church, and a roughly hewn town hall which was called the Proprietors' House. Because no newspaper reached the village, the townspeople had to depend on news filtered through the blacksmith shop, the hub of information and the gossip center.

In the spring of that year when Martha and Gordon were married, she was thirty-one and he was thirty. Their wedding had been postponed for several years while Gordon was off fighting in the Revolution as an officer serving under General Horatio Gates in the New York campaign. He returned home broken in health from exposure and injuries suffered on the battlefield. In spite of his poor condition, Gordon decided to try his hand at homesteading on virgin timberland, four hundred acres in the township of Newport situated on the Sunapee side of East Mountain, about two miles from the center of the village.

The Buells' farm overlooked the lovely verdant valley where the Sugar River is fed by the outlet waters of Lake Sunapee. Their one-and-a-half-story farmhouse was typically New England colonial in the simplicity of its lines. It was on this pleasant farm that Sarah was born on October 24, 1788. Her parents must have been pleased with a first daughter, for they already had two sons, Charles and Horatio. Sarah was four when her sister Martha was born. The children grew up with close family ties fostered by the shared chores and activities of farm life. Farming frequently involves the entire family, and this was never more true than in pioneer America.

At the time Sarah was growing up in Newport, formal education was sketchy at best for boys and nonexistent for girls; however, she received an amazingly good education at home. Her mother would gather the youngsters around the dining room table or, in the cold weather, around the hearthstone and teach them to read from the *Bible* and *The Pilgrim's Progress*, stressing strong moral principles along with their ABCs. Martha Buell was an excellent teacher with a keen mind and a retentive memory. She was also a born story teller and inspired Sarah with a love of literature that was to last a lifetime.

It was no traumatic experience for Sarah when her oldest brother Charles left for his lessons at the Proprietors' House because she still had Horatio at home with her. Horatio was only nineteen months her senior and the two were alike in many ways; they were apt pupils with well matched abilities, sharing many interests. But when her favorite brother went off to school and she learned that only boys were allowed to attend, it was very difficult for her to understand why. Perhaps the seeds of her long crusade for equal educational opportunities for girls were sown in early childhood when she was unable to share Horatio's school experiences. However, thanks to her gifted mother she did not fall behind her brother in his studies.

Sarah, a precocious reader, showed uncommon motivation at an early age. Two books she read before turning eleven: at age seven *The Mysteries of Udolpho* by Anne Radcliffe and when she was ten Ramsey's *History of the American Revolution*. These impressed her so much that they inspired two of her earliest aims in life. Anne Radcliffe's Gothic romance was the sort of book she liked to take to her favorite nook under a hazel tree beside the Sugar River. There, curled up on a mossy bank, how her heart must have pounded as she read about the frightening experiences of the lovely

Emily St. Aubert who was separated from her fiance, the handsome and debonair Valencourt, and locked by her ruthless uncle in the ancient castle of Udolpho, a dark and mysterious place of weird and supernatural terrors. This was the first novel she had read and it was written by a woman! As young as she was, Sarah had noticed that few books she had seen were written by Americans and *none* by an American woman. "The wish to promote the reputation of my own sex, and to do something for my own country, was among the earliest mental emotions I can recollect. This love of country was deeply engraved on my heart, by reading, when I was not more than ten years old, Ramsey's 'History of the American Revolution.' It made me a patriot for life." Much of her later editorial work would reflect this strong love of her native land.

At the turn of the century, the village of Newport was only thirty-five years old, but the population had swelled from the original thirty-three settlers in 1767 to over eight hundred inhabitants. The rapidly growing town was gaining a measure of sophistication. One milestone of progress came when a weekly newspaper named the *Farmers Museum*, delivered by carrier from Walpole, New Hampshire, provided news of a much broader scope than could be gleaned from the blacksmith shop. Attractive homes of many wealthy and influential families stretched along the main street which was lined with Lombardy poplars. A Town Hall had been built on the southeast side of the four corners at the foot of Claremont Hill, and clustered around this intersection were the stores and shops. The white tower of the Congregational Church added a touch of dignity to the scenic town in its valley setting surrounded by rolling hills and nearby wooded mountains.

In 1800 Sarah was twelve but she seemed more mature than her years because of the adult books she had read; books by Milton, Addison, Pope, Johnson, Cowper, Burns, and Shakespeare. While she was gaining knowledge through reading, Horatio was studying with the Congregational minister, a man who tutored young men in college preparatory studies. Sarah's brother planned to attend Dartmouth College, a logical choice because the school was only thirty miles from Newport. Having to rely on the horse for transportation and the extremely poor road conditions made distance an important factor.

With an insatiable inner drive to learn all she possibly could,

Sarah studied Horatio's subjects with him, but once more the doors to formal education were closed to her. Her brother felt badly about the unhappy situation and tried to do as much as he could to correct the unfair sex discrimination by setting up a study routine for Sarah and tutoring her during his long school vacations. This method worked out so well that when he was graduated with top honors in 1809, through her reading and his tutoring, Sarah had received the equivalence of a college education, lacking only the diploma.

Shortly after Horatio entered Dartmouth, Sarah began teaching young boys and *girls* in a small school not far from her home. This was a private school and Sarah was paid by the parents of her pupils. She took the position in part to help her father with his financial burdens, for Gordon was finding farming increasingly difficult. Age had put a further strain on his never-too-rugged constitution. Sarah was a born teacher and her school was very progressive both in the subjects taught and her method of presentation. Her students were drilled on the three "R's" but also studied some higher mathematics, read from the classics, and learned a smattering of Latin. Sarah taught her youngsters to think for themselves while many schools still relied on the rote method of teaching.

It was at this small school that the incident involving "Mary's Lamb" is reputed to have taken place. Sarah was surprised one morning to see one of her students, a girl named Mary, enter the classroom followed by her pet lamb. The visitor was far too distracting to be permitted to remain in the building and so Sarah "turned him out." The lamb stayed nearby till school was dismissed and then ran up to Mary looking for attention and protection. The other youngsters wanted to know why the lamb loved Mary so much and their teacher explained it was because Mary loved her pet. Then Sarah used the incident to get a moral across to the class.

And you each gentle animal,
In confidence may bind,
And make them answer to your call,
If you are always *kind*.

Sarah was still teaching school in 1810 when it became evident that a change in the life style of the Buell family was necessary because her father could no longer continue farming. Gordon decided to try his hand at an entirely different business. The Buells built a small inn, the Rising Sun Tavern, in the center of Newport at the foot of East Mountain and moved there from the farm in the spring of 1811. The name chosen for the venture is interesting because the inn faced the west and the setting sun. Perhaps their hopes for success in the enterprise were as optimistic as the promise of a new day with the rising sun. If so, these hopes were soon dashed. Three tragedies within a short span of time struck deeply at the heart of the family, literally cutting their numbers in half.

Horatio was studying for the law, but his brother Charles had chosen a different path, answering the call of the sea. This decision proved a fatal one for he was lost at sea before turning twenty-seven, leaving a young wife and two small daughters. Then on November 25, 1811, Sarah's sister Martha was a victim of pulmonary tuberculosis. She was only eighteen. One month later on Christmas morning Sarah's mother died. Gordon was heartbroken. All the great hopes for success and happiness at the Rising Sun had been ground into dust, and he had neither the strength nor the will to continue with the business now that his wife was no longer at his side. He sold the tavern in the spring after operating the business for only one year.

The ill-fated venture did have one fortunate result. The inn was the place where Sarah met her future husband. David Hale had just opened an office in Newport and was working hard to establish a successful law practice. During a two-year courtship, Sarah continued teaching. She and her father lived in rooms at the Rising Sun, and it was there her marriage to David took place on the twenty-third of October, 1813, one day before the bride's twenty-fifth birthday.

2 Family Life

The Hales' home on Main Street was in the newer section of
Newport center just north of the well-established residential area
with the dignified homes of the founding fathers. The two-story
white frame house, set back from the street and shaded by tall oak
and beautiful maple trees, was directly across from the level
stretch of land that today is the Town Common. Then it was a
marshy spot with large patches of tufted grass among little winding rivulets. To get from one side to the other oldsters stepped,
and youngsters jumped, from one small green island to the next.
On warm summer evenings Sarah and David were serenaded by
crickets in concert with the rhythmical croaking of frogs thriving
in the muddy bottom of the miniature streams.

Sarah thought her home was just perfect—comfortable,
roomy enough for raising a family, and yet with an air of
stateliness befitting a lawyer with a promising future. The appearance of stateliness was accentuated by an artistic fanlight over
the front door. A wide hallway ran back from this entrance
through the center of the house to another door leading to the kitchen. There were two large front rooms on each side of the hall.
The one on the left was a formal parlor reserved for special occa-
sions, but the homey and colorfully decorated keeping room to the
right was the family living room. The focal point of the keeping
room was a handsome fireplace with a mantlepiece adorned with
favorite knick-knacks and, in the summertime, with bowls of
flowers from Sarah's garden. Beside a cherry table drawn up

before the fireplace were two comfortable armchairs. It was obvious that David and Sarah loved books, for over a writing desk was a large bookcase filled with well-worn volumes. Sarah's sewing table, a wooden clock, and an assortment of chairs completed the furniture in this most pleasant room.

There was nothing the couple enjoyed more at the end of the day than to settle down in front of the fireplace to read or study together by lamplight in the relaxed atmosphere of the keeping room, a custom they continued even after their children were born. As intimate as these evenings were, they did not dress informally. There was no telephone to give warning of the unexpected, the possibility of friends dropping by, or a client stopping in to consult with David.

Sarah, an attractive brunette of average height, was well proportioned and wore floor-length dresses with closely fitted waist and low neckline which showed off her figure. Large hazel eyes, rimmed with long thick lashes, were her most outstanding feature. David was almost six feet tall, a good-looking man in his white high-collared shirt and dark dinner jacket.

When the couple began their habit of studying in the evening hours, David was continuing the unique pattern of Sarah's education intiated by Horatio. He taught his wife world history, French, and a relatively new subject, botany. Sarah like to write and David encouraged her in this hobby and helped improve her style by stressing the effectiveness of simple but forceful English as opposed to the flowery verbosity so popular in that century.

At first Sarah was very unsure about her writing ability and David found a way to give her more self-confidence. He submitted some of her work to Newport's weekly newspaper, the *New Hampshire Spectator*. When Cyrus Barton, the editor-owner, willingly agreed to publish some of her stories and poems, Sarah's belief in her ability grew and her reputation as a writer spread in the local area.

The self-confidence thus gained led to another outlet for her interest in writing. Many literary clubs were springing up across the country. Some, especially those in large cities, were highly sophisticated cultural lyceums whose members paid top fees to secure capable and well-known lecturers. Newport's Coterie, headed by Sarah, was far less pretentious.

The club members were some of her young adult friends who met on pleasant afternoons on a natural terrace overlooking "the bend," a branch of the Sugar River winding through a green meadow dotted with clumps of hazel and white birch. The gathering place was under the spreading branches of the "Matrimonial Tree." This "tree" was actually two giant elms growing so closely together that their lofty branches intertwined to form what the club members called "a reciprocal embrace." To the young people the trees symbolized the joining by marriage of two individuals into one union.

The Coterie had two main purposes. Sarah hoped they could all gain cultural knowledge by reading aloud and by discussing current magazine articles and books. The other purpose was to help aspiring authors of prose, poetry, and drama improve their writing skills through group criticism of their works. These were read aloud or acted out with the setting provided by nature. Tables and benches were scattered around in shady spots, and in the late afternoon the delightful aroma of wood smoke filled the lazy summer air. Tea brewed over the open fire was served with small cakes and sandwiches while lively conversation followed by song fests added enjoyment to the simple social gatherings.

Some of the club members had the thrill of seeing the fruits of their effort in print in the *Spectator*. One might think these budding authors would also have wished to see their names in the paper, but in keeping with the popular trend of the day, they usually hid their identities under pseudonyms—a single letter of the alphabet or a name taken from the classics or the Bible. Who were Philo, Mercurius, Minerva, Rebecca, or Uncle Toby? The identity of one pen name has survived: Thirza was the name chosen by Sarah's sister-in-law, Hannah Hale. Later Hannah would marry the owner-editor of the *Spectator* and become Mrs. Cyrus Barton.

In 1818 David and Sarah had been married for almost five years and had two sons, David and Horatio. By late summer Sarah knew she was pregnant again. Perhaps this time they would be happily surprised with a daughter. The pattern of their marriage was smooth and pleasant—complete compatibility, a lovely home in a congenial rural town, David's successful law practice, two loving and well-loved sons, and the added bonus of many close friends—what more could any couple desire? Sarah always had hired help for household chores which gave her some leisure time for her hobbies. There appeared to be no dark cloud on her horizon. However, she suddenly came down with an illness diagnosed as pulmonary tuberculosis, the same dread disease that had robbed her sister Martha of life seven years earlier. Because there was no known cure, their doctor could hold out no hope for her recovery. Sarah's deep religious belief in eternity helped her face death stoically, but the thought of parting from David and her two small sons caused her great anguish. Then too, was the new life which had quickened within her doomed to die with her? The only person who refused to abandon hope was David.

One evening in the fall of that year, he was reading aloud to Sarah who was reclining on the keeping room sofa. Suddenly jumping to his feet and without a word to his sick wife, he dropped the book onto the table and rushed out of the house. The utter despair of watching Sarah's life fading away must have mounted to such a pitch that he could no longer stand the strain. His sudden departure puzzled and alarmed Sarah. Where had he gone and why? Several hours elapsed before he returned.

Then when David did come back, his strange behavior surprised his wife even more. He strode across the room, picked her up in his arms and held her close saying with great emotion "Listen, you are not going to die! I won't let you!"

David never told Sarah where he spent those long troubled hours but did explain his plan to save her life. He held out hope of a cure on two counts. First, he was a firm believer that fresh air is usually beneficial to health, especially in the case of sick lungs. Perhaps breathing the pure autumn air might help Sarah recover. Also he had heard of a "grape cure." Frost grapes grew in abundance in the pastures, over the stone walls and along the roadsides in New Hampshire. They were called frost grapes because on the first nippy night, this native fruit turned a reddish color. Whether eating plentifully of these wild grapes could really help cure his wife was questionable at best and yet the hopelessness of the situation called for desperate measures.

David hastily arranged his business affairs so that he could put his plan into action the very next day. His sister, Hannah, agreed to stay with the children while he took Sarah on an extended trip through the New Hampshire mountains. Before leaving town they stopped their gig in front of the doctor's house to tell their friend about the plans. He tried to dissuade David, saying he was convinced Sarah would not return alive. In spite of this solemn warning, the couple set off hoping against hope that they could prove their friend wrong, that Sarah could win out over death.

Autumn in New Hampshire is a magical time of the year when nature splashes the landscape with a gay exuberance of color. Was there some magic, too, in the clusters of grapes growing over the countryside? Some magic in the crystal air? Were their prayers for a miracle answered? Whatever the cause, Sarah returned home completely cured. She herself gave much of the credit to the frost grapes, and for the rest of her life she always kept grapes on hand even when they were out of season and expensive.

After Sarah regained her strength, life returned to normal and the evening studying was resumed. The following March she gave birth to a daughter, Frances Ann, but joy was mixed with sadness because her father died the same spring. Twenty months later a second daughter was born, and David named the baby, Sarah Josepha, after her mother; she was called Josepha to avoid the confusion of two Sarahs. In 1821 David was elected Worshipful Master of the Corinthian Lodge of the Masons and was serving a second term when fate dealt the Hale family a cruel blow.

On a cool but sunny day in late September David had an appointment with a client in Fishersfield (now Newbury)—a small town at the south end of Lake Sunapee. When he climbed into his gig and headed for the Bradford stage road which went over East Mountain, there was no threat of an early wintry storm in the crisp air. The dirt road which ran past the farm where Sarah was born cut through wild forest land which was broken only by scattered farms carved out of the mountainside. The trees along the way were turning autumn yellow, orange, and red. Some of the maples were completely crimson, but a few trees still wore summer green. Wood smoke from the farmhouses spoke of the coming of winter.

On the Sunapee side of East Mountain increasing cloudiness robbed the colored leaves of their luster. David hoped that his business in Fishersfield would be taken care of in short order;

however, this was not to be. By late afternoon he was anxious to get started for home. Heavy gray clouds that darkened the sky looked ominous. There was the feel of snow in the air. In spite of the threatening weather David turned down an invitation to spend the night, for he knew Sarah would be concerned about him.

The fierce fury of an exceptionally early snow storm hit with full force just as David rounded the curve at the base of Mount Sunapee. The covered gig did not protect him from wind-whipped snow blowing in through the open sides. His horse slowed to a walk as the visibility became so poor that it was difficult to distinguish the edge of the snow-dusted road from the white world around it. By the time David reached his yard at the end of the bitter cold trip, he was chilled to the bone. Dry clothes, warm food and drink, and a fire blazing on the open hearth did little to lessen his chills. David went to bed after supper not dreaming he would never be a well man again. Pneumonia set in and he died on September 25, 1822, just two weeks before the birth of his son William.

The shock of his sudden death was almost unbearable for Sarah, who felt that with his loss every earthly hope had perished. To compound the pathetic situation, she found herself in financial straits. Her husband's successful law practice had provided the family with every comfort; however, "he had hardly reached the age when men of his profession begin to lay up property" and she was left poor.

David's funeral service was conducted by the members of the Corinthian Lodge, and he was buried in the Pine Street Cemetery overlooking the village of Newport. In her home below the hill, his widow mourned his death and yearned for his advice, wondering what he would suggest as a way out of her unhappy predicament. Her main concern was for the children and their support—not about whether they should "inherit wealth, but to be deprived of the advantages of education was to make them 'poor indeed.' " David had always been the decision maker. What would he tell her to do now?

The avenues for remunerative employment for women were few—mainly dressmaking, millinery, and teaching. One of her early biographers stated, "Why Mrs. Hale did not return to her teaching nobody knows." The answer is the simple one of dollars and cents. Job availability was limited because women had not been generally accepted in the public school system. Even if Sarah had decided to go in that direction, it is highly doubtful that she could have supported her children on the meager salary of a teacher. The payment made to male teachers was small, and women sometimes earned as little as half as much salary for a comparable position. Teaching was out.

In the midst of her quandary David did come to her rescue, in an indirect way—through his fellow Masons. The members of the Lodge voted not to elect a Worshipful Master to replace David for a full year, proof of their high regard for him. They gave further evidence of their affection and esteem by offering to set Sarah and her sister-in-law, Hannah, up in the millinery business, temporarily solving the problem of family support for David's young widow.

3   The Birth
of an Editor

Open for business. By spring the new milliners were ready for customers and so they placed an advertisement in the May sixteenth edition of the *Spectator* for their "new fancy goods and millinery—brown cambricks, figured gauze, silk mourning bonnets, caps and head-dress of the latest and most approved patterns" just received from Boston and New York. Sarah and Hannah promised their customers "constant attention and cheerful attendance." In the beginning both women were excited about the enterprise; however, it soon became evident that only one of them was genuinely suited to the profession. The venture proved to be providential for Hannah who is listed in town records as Newport's first successful milliner, but for her sister-in-law it was quite a different matter.

When Hannah finished one of her elegant creations, striking just the right touch with well-placed feathers or contrasting colored bows, she was delighted with her achievement. How very much Sarah wished she could feel the same enthusiasm. Instead, a job completed just brought a sigh of relief with her only pleasure coming from the knowledge that payment for her work meant food on the table or clothes for the children. Her talents and interest lay along different lines.

Whenever she could snatch a few moments, Sarah would slip away to the keeping room to work on a novel she had started shortly after William's birth or to compose poetry. As the days lengthened into weeks and summer came to Newport, her desire for more time to spend on her writing turned the millinery work into pure drudgery. Her most productive times were in the evenings, but sometimes she would even write with William on her lap—awkward but preferable to not writing at all.

Before David's death she had written a number of poems, and soon she had enough to comprise a small book of verse. The problem was how to get them published, a knotty problem indeed for a relatively unknown author. Luck was with her. The Masons came to her assistance for the second time within a year by offering to pay for publishing *The Genius of Oblivion and Other Original Poems* written "By a Lady of New Hampshire." This little volume had popular appeal, although none of the poems warranted literary recognition. Yet this first book was sufficiently successful to enable the striving author to abandon the millinery business, or rather to leave it in Hannah's capable hands, and to begin writing in earnest. With her new-found freedom, Sarah spent a great deal of time on her novel, *Northwood.* She did not limit her effort to this project alone but tried submitting some of her work to popular magazines and she met with immediate success. Three periodicals accepted contributions the first year; the *Atlantic Monthly,* the *Literary Gazette,* and Boston's *Spectator and Ladies' Album* — and she also entered and won a number of poetry contests. Then in 1826 alone the *Spectator and Ladies' Album* printed seventeen of her poems, two short stories, and a literary review. The following year it was a feather in her cap to have four poems included in a small gift book, *The Memorial.* Gift books were exceedingly fashionable, and *The Memorial* was one of the best.

Northwood was progressing well and nearing completion. Part of the novel was set in her native state and part in the South; the name was taken from an actual New Hampshire town that lies on the road running from Concord to Portsmouth.

As Sarah contrasted life in the North with conditions in the South, she showed familiarity with her subject matter when depicting northern places and customs; however, her descriptions of southern scenes and ways lack authenticity. Details of contemporary life in the post-Colonial era in New England were well handled. She sincerely hoped the story would become a source of information for future generations of Americans and that "A century hence, when our country boasts tens of millions of in-habitants . . ., this unpretending book may be a reference describ-ing faithfully the age when to be industrious was to be respectable." This wish failed; her writing style was cloaked too heavily in the Victorian vernacular for present-day tastes.

Industrious was the key word. "There can be no excellency without industry. The mind of the idle, like the garden of the slothful, will be overgrown with briars and thorns; and indolence, under whatever fashionable name... is a more dangerous enemy to practical goodness and to moral improvement, than even dissipa-tion.... Those who tread a devious path may possibly retrace their steps, or even by a circuitous route finally reach their goal; but those who never stir, how can they win the race!"

During the summer of 1826 Sarah went to Boston to talk with the publishers, Bowles and Dearborn, who had shown an interest in her novel. While in the city she stopped in to see the editor of the *Spectator*. She wanted to thank in person the man who had published more of her early work than anyone else. Later this editor reported in the gossip column of his magazine that he had been given the privilege of reading her *Northwood* manuscript. He was so highly impressed with her talent that he followed the pro-gress of the book with great interest, commenting from time to time about it in the *Spectator and Ladies' Album*. Then in the April 1827 edition he said that Sarah was surrounded by her children and was constantly interrupted by business of a "very anti-literary nature."

During the day distractions did press in from every side and there were moments when Sarah wondered if she could ever become an author; but in the evening when she sat writing at the keeping-room table across from an empty armchair, the room must have seemed too large, too quiet with the only sounds the scratching of her quill pen across the paper and the gentle rustling of the open hearth fire whispering to her of happier days.

Early in December of 1827 Sarah did emerge when *North-wood* was published in two volumes by Bowles and Dearborn. The success of the novel was instantaneous. Press and magazine reviews were enthusiastic and one notice in particular pleased Sarah. Bryant stated in the *Literary Gazette* that *Northwood* was proof that neither talent nor material was wanting in our country.

The book was a trend setter—perhaps the first novel to use the national scene as background for a story. It was certainly the first novel of consequence by an American woman, and the first to deal forthrightly with the question of slavery, a subject other writers either skirted or avoided entirely. When Sarah pointed out the economic as well as the moral roots of the mammoth problem, she predated Harriet Beecher Stowe by twenty-five years. She chose the theme out of her great concern that the slavery issue might tear her beloved country apart. She hoped that a book sympathetic to both sections, pointing out the dangers of the ever-widening gulf between the northerners and their southern compatriots, might bring about a better understanding and contribute to the most important consideration of all, the preservation of the Union.

Northwood proved to be the instrument that sent Sarah to Boston and into the field of journalism. Many congratulatory letters and promises of aid came by stage to Newport less than a month after the novel was published. One was from the Reverend John Lauris Blake, an Episcopal clergyman, asking Sarah to accept the position of editor for a new publication, a proposed periodical exclusively for women. The only stipulation was that she would have to move to Boston. This offer took her completely by surprise. To be asked to speak to and for women across the nation when only a few years before she had been an unknown writer from a small New Hampshire village was an unexpected honor and a great challenge, and yet she found the decision to accept the proposal the most difficult of her entire life.

Acceptance of the offer would, or at least *should*, make it possible to realize her dream of sending all five of her youngsters to college; however, it would also necessitate leaving David, Horatio, and the girls with relatives. The support and education of her children, not a desire for fame, convinced Sarah that she should take the editorial position.

The thought of this separation weighed heavily on her mind and Sarah postponed the move to Boston till March by editing the new *Ladies' Magazine* from Newport. The keeping room became her office and the lamp burned late into the night as she thoughtfully planned the prospectus of the periodical for the first edition; composed articles, poems, and stories; edited the work of others; and fulfilled all the million and one requirements to complete the magazine. An end to her procrastination came when she found the task impossible from such a great distance.

David was only thirteen and yet he was already doing preparatory work for entering West Point. When he went to the Academy the following year, he was the youngest member of the freshman class. Young Horatio was sent to Glen Falls, New York, to live with Sarah's brother, Horatio Buell, who was an outstanding man, a well-known lawyer, and an influential politician. The children had another uncle who distinguished himself in several fields. David Hale's younger brother, Selma. He also was a prominent lawyer and politician as well as being a printer, editor, and historian. Nine-year-old Frances and seven-year-old Josepha went to stay with their Uncle Selma Hale and his family in Keene, New Hampshire. William, five and a half, was the only child to remain with his mother.

Although Sarah had been a widow for almost six years, she still dressed in black and continued to do so for the rest of her life. Her sincere devotion to David's memory is unquestionable, but she also found black becoming. Sarah had a good figure, but she always yearned to be a little taller than her *almost* medium height. Because of this, she held her head high hoping to give the appearance of adding inches to her stature—and she found wearing black did make her look taller! Black also accentuated her white skin in a very becoming way.

Long before departure day arrived, Newport was buzzing with the pros and cons of a woman setting out to seek her livelihood in a big city. Many who gathered at the stage stop in front of the Rising Sun had grave misgivings about the wisdom of Sarah's decision, yet all admired her courage and determination to succeed. She looked so vulnerable—a slight figure in black. Were there tears in her eyes as she helped young William up into the stagecoach? Tears perhaps, and yet the sadness was mixed with the exciting thrill of adventure felt by every pioneer taking a giant step into a new world.

4   Boston, 1828

Sarah found the long trip from Newport to Boston wearing. It was difficult to appreciate the loveliness of the landscape's fresh greenery while being bounced and tossed from side to side as the stagecoach traveled over deeply rutted dirt roads often muddied by heavy spring rains. For a five-year-old, especially one with William's energetic enthusiasm, the journey was bound to be exciting. When his mother was not answering his seemingly endless questions or telling him a story to quiet his restlessness, she thought about the miles that were separating her from hometown friends and relatives and wondered about her reception in Boston. Sarah did not question the wisdom of her decision and was actually looking forward to taking charge of "her" magazine in person, but her uncertainities about the future are understandable. At a later date she said that she had expected to be surrounded by strangers, but found instead sympathetic friends.

Boston with its golden-domed State House was an intriguing blend of contrasts in the spring of 1828—winding narrow streets with horse-drawn wagons and coaches rumbling over the cobblestones, fancy gigs and ornate carriages, merchants in their dark broadcloth suits hurrying past noisy street vendors crying out their wares, lovely ladies with full skirts brushing the pavements, strolling beneath their parasols, sedate brick houses aloof on Beacon Hill overlooking cattle grazing on the green slope of the Common, and white church spires cutting the blue of the sky. Boston then as Boston now had color and character, but in 1828 the city was much smaller in area and its pulse was the tides of the sea.

Before hundreds of acres of man-made land and many tall buildings robbed the city dwellers of the sight, of the sound and of the salty taste of the ocean, Bostonians could look out over their harbor and see the straight masts and white sails of clipper ships returning from Europe, Africa, Asia, South America, and the West Indies as they slipped past the myriads of harbor islands to lie at anchor by Long Wharf, Central, or India. The magnificent seaport with its large warehouses, numerous stores and over two hundred docks comprised about one third of the metropolis. The new editor was exchanging her mountain scenery and quiet way of life for a busy city by the sea.

The early part of the nineteenth century was a period of tremendous change. At the same time that the country was rapidly expanding westward, steam was bringing remote areas closer together. A spurt of transportation improvements saw many new bridges and canals built, harbors dredged, new roads laid out and old ones made better. At the rate civilization was pushing back the frontiers, it appeared that the nation might one day extend all the way to the Pacific Ocean. Harvard College students that year debated the question whether one man could *be President* of the United States when it will eventually be settled from the Atlantic to Pacific—a situation almost beyond the realm of imagination at that time.

Boston was changing, too. Before the turn of the century the section of the city bordering on Washington Street (then Marlborough Street) was considered very elite; however, after Bulfinch started building homes for wealthy Bostonians on Beacon Hill and in the West End, the older part changed character and many of the large homes became rooming or boarding houses. On narrow side streets, quiet and respectable, tree-shaded houses were set back from the road in small gardens guarded by picket fences. Sarah found lodgings in this area within walking distance of her office at Putnam and Hunt, 41 Washington Street.

Her small suite of rooms included a living room which doubled as a writing room in the evening. Sarah and William ate their meals with the other boarders in a large dining hall on the first floor. The other gathering place was the heavily draped and ornately decorated parlor. During the first year of adjustment, Sarah could not spend much time being sociable except on Sundays.

Church in the morning was followed by dinner and then an afternoon with William at the Frog Pond in the Common or visiting with friends. Late in the afternoon she frequently joined the other boarders in the parlor for tea and conversation.

The first problem to be settled on arrival had to do with William's education and care while she was at work. Sarah hired a teacher—"hired" with the payment being the use of her living room for a small school, so the teacher could instruct other neighborhood children along with William. The children's education was carried out under Sarah's thoughtful and competent guidance. The specific arrangements she made for her son's care while neither she nor the teacher was in charge are unknown, but it would seem likely that some woman in the boarding house may have been paid for this service.

The demands of her new position gave Sarah far less time than she wished to be with William. At night after he was tucked into bed, she sat at her living room desk and wrote—rewrote, edited, and composed for the magazine—all in longhand. Each word had to be precise, just right. How tired her hands must have been at the end of the evening and how her head and back must have ached from this tedious work. Sometimes she would be up late enough to hear through the open window the watchman's cry "Twelve o'clock. The night is fair and all's well!" or his frantic "Fire!" followed by the clanging of engines as they raced by as fast as the horses could pull them.

No matter at what hour she retired, Sarah had to be up early so she could get William ready for the day and have sufficient time left for her own careful grooming. In those first Boston years money was scarce, and yet Sarah always dressed attractively. Her favorite material for city living was silk "because it shook the dust." Her black gowns were trimmed with white lace at the throat and wrist—simple but elegant.

One of the first of the sympathetic friends who welcomed her on arrival was the clergyman John Blake, the man who had written about the editorial position. This rector and Sarah had a number of things in common; both were from New Hampshire, they were the same age, and they shared a deep interest in furthering the cause of women. John Blake had been in charge of a Concord, New Hampshire, church when he decided to take positive action in behalf of women by establishing a very successful school for girls. When he was transferred to St. Matthew's Church in Boston, he moved his school to the city and fulfilled the dual roles of parish minister and the headmaster of Cornhill School for Young Ladies. The idea of a quality magazine for women seems to have been his, and he helped with the publication of the *Ladies' Magazine*. His friendship and assistance meant a great deal to Sarah.

One of the first contributors to the magazine was Lydia Child, another pioneer editor but one in magazines for children. She was in charge of the *Juvenile Miscellany*, also printed by Putnam and Hunt, and was in an excellent position to give many tips to Sarah, a big help to a novice.

In 1828 there were in Boston a large number of good and widely circulated periodicals headed by very capable men. Some of the best known were the *Sentinel* under Benjamin Russell, the *Galaxy* edited by Joseph Buckingham, and the *North American Review* managed by the illustrious Edward Everett. These were primarily aimed at a male market though some devoted a few pages to women. The *Spectator and Ladies' Album*, so helpful to Sarah during her literary debut, was for both sexes till it changed hands and name that year, becoming the *Bower of Taste* edited by Katherine Ware who made it a weekly periodical for women. Her journal and Sarah's were not the first to cater to women, but no previous attempt had lasted longer than five years.

Women's magazines before Sarah's had offered sentimental poems and stories with exotic Gothic or Oriental settings. The bulk of the content was snipped from other sources, and the men publishing these were referred to as "scissors editors." The *Bower of Taste* was modeled on these earlier publications, but Sarah aimed higher, intending to instruct as well as entertain. The task she set herself was a great challenge, and she did not underestimate its magnitude.

The publishing firm of Putnam and Hunt had only recently come into being when John Putnam formed a partnership with Freeman Hunt. Their business was in the same building with Marsh, Capen and Lyon, a firm of booksellers and publishers, and

Putnam and Hunt did much of the printing for this neighboring business. At that time most of the book-related industries were congregated on a half-mile stretch of Washington Street from the Old State House to the Old South Church. Quaint book stores with protruding windows with leaded panes were sandwiched among publishing firms, printers and engravers, and book binders—a book lover's paradise with old world charm and glamour.

The *Ladies' Magazine* came out on the fifteenth of the month, contained about thirty pages, and cost three dollars for a year's subscription. One problem connected with successfully launching the new endeavor plagued Sarah from the onset. Knowing only too well that the man of the family held the purse strings, she pondered the question—"How can I win his support?" Her solution was a novel approach to magazine advertising. Always a diplomat, often a strategist, and not infrequently a schemer, she showed her flair for gentle and discrete management by enticing the American man into giving her magazine a chance.

In her appeal to men in the "Introduction" of the initial January 1828 number, she asked the busy husband who was forced to leave his wife alone at home if he would not "rejoice that he had it in his power to afford her the means of agreeably beguiling the interval of his absence?" A subscription to the *Ladies' Magazine* would give him this opportunity to please his wife, and the editor assured him "that nothing found on the pages of this publication, shall cause her to be the less assiduous in preparing for his reception, or less sincere in welcoming his return."

To fathers she promised that nothing in the magazine would in any way weaken parental authority or "disturb family concord." Then to "The lover, aye, the favored lover—on him we confidently depend for support." Sarah was relying on him to present "the lady of his love" with a gift subscription as token of his esteem, knowing that she would think of him fondly as she read it for enjoyment and to improve her mind. A bit overdone perhaps, but Sarah was appealing to the sentimental Victorian and her sales pitch met with great success.

Much closer to her heart than the necessary advertising was the magazine content, and she told her new public that her first concern was to promote the reputation of her sex through better educational opportunities. "Even before I went to Boston," she wrote at a later date, "I asked a friend to insert in the first number of the publication an article which would strike this keynote; and, from that time until the *Ladies' Magazine* was merged with a larger publication, there was not one volume of it which did not abound in appeals, in arguments, stories, songs and criticism bearing upon the subject of feminine education."

The prospectus for the new magazine was set forth by Sarah in the "Introduction"—there were to be sketches of American scenery and customs, critical reviews of current literature, biographical essays, anecdotes about eminent women and "whatever is calculated to illustrate and improve the female character." She said that the "work will be national— American—and well written communications, whether poems, letters, sketches, tales, or essays, descriptive of American scenery, character, and manners, will be welcome to its pages."

With this emphasis on local and national material, Sarah made a great contribution to American writing. When her "Introduction" stated that she wanted native talent and original work, she was taking a stand against the common practice of periodical and book publishers of "stealing" from English authors and each other, a practice she considered objectionable and dishonest. Insisting on original work, though, put a heavy load on Sarah, especially during the first two years of publication.

The last few pages were reserved for Sarah's editorial department. Here she gave notices of magazine policy, corresponded with contributors and subscribers, took further opportunity to elevate the stature of women, and she also sponsored many worthwhile causes.

The first cause to be sponsored was the Fatherless and Widow's Society of Boston, a new organization set up by some of the city's well-to-do women to help ease the financial burdens of widows and their children, a pet cause Sarah would promote for many years. Including this in the first volume of the *Ladies' Magazine* was the finishing touch that set the stage for all future issues because Sarah laid down the base of her three-pronged editorial thrust—the promotion of educational opportunities for her sex; the encouragement of authors, especially women, to write about their own localities with the inclusion of national themes and scenes; and the sponsorship of worthwhile causes. This was an innovative approach because these fields had not been dealt with to any extent in either weekly or monthly periodicals. Sarah was only thirty-nine years old when she set out on this new course in journalism—a widow with no previous editorial experience.

5 Ladies'
Magazine

The circulation of the *Ladies' Magazine* had grown so fast the first year that Sarah and her publishers knew they were right in assuming that there were many women hungry for more than just simple fiction and household hints in their literary menu. These women were looking for information, advice, and encouragement, and their editor was delighted to cater to their needs. In January 1829 she began a series entitled "Authoresses" with an article which stated that if national self-government hoped to remain successful and permanent, there must be national education for girls as well as boys.

Another essay in the same issue stated Sarah's belief in the basic differences between the sexes. She felt strongly that women as a whole exceed men in moral strength. Her contention was that whereas men are much stronger physically, women must therefore be stronger in a moral and religious sense. That men are given more physical strength is, excepting the mythical Amazons, unquestionably true; but the assertion that therefore women inherit a stiffer moral fiber is debatable. Women are set apart by their role in the reproduction cycle. Sarah, who would have scoffed at the uni-sex concept, believed that the roles of the sexes are of equal importance but different, a position she would reiterate many times during her long editorial career.

In stressing the differing spheres of the sexes, it was never her intention to place woman on a pedestal. Her goal was to see her sex educated and woman's stature elevated so she could take her rightful place as an equal—*beside* man, not *above* him.

In the January 1829 issue there was also a request for more original poems, stories, and articles because "It must be borne in mind, that this periodical is not a compilation, a mere 'omnium gatherum' of the shreds and clippings of all the old newspapers in the nation." Originality was a prerequisite to acceptance yet not the sole criterion. "Why," she asked, "is it that persons, who converse with propriety on many subjects, when attempting to place their ideas on paper, fail so miserably? Because they will not write as they would speak. They imagine they must have a lofty theme, and long words and pompous descriptions. We never read such, without feeling inclined to use Burchell's exclamation—Fudge!"

Sarah's request for more contributions came about because there were so many demands on her time that attempting to write for the magazine as well as edit it had become a monumental task. In time other women would be inspired to join in her effort to further their role in the field of literature, but for a few years Sarah worked almost completely on her own. She composed almost half of the magazine content. Month after month she struggled to meet deadlines without compromising on the quality of the *Ladies' Magazine*. A few faithful contributors were Lydia Sigourney, Sarah Whitman, Lydia Child, Elmira Hunt, and Maria Fuller.

For the first two years as editor Sarah was given a free hand in making policy decisions for *her* magazine, and yet almost from the first one of her firm opinions was questioned. She was convinced there was no place in a quality periodical for fashion prints even though their inclusion was bound to increase sales. The majority of subscribers had no fault to find with her policy; however, some readers missed the features they had come to expect in a woman's magazine—recipes and embroidery patterns, and they also asked for a fashion column with illustrations to be included on a regular basis. Sarah was most reluctant to compromise with the high moral and intellectual tone of the magazine, and she fought vigorously against the growing demand for fashion plates.

These popular fashion illustrations, imported from England, first appeared in America when the *Boston Atheneum* introduced them to the reading public in their October 1828 volume. This highly sophisticated periodical made the uncharacteristic move with the hope of increasing sales, the same motive which forced Sarah to capitulate in November of 1830.

Losing a fight can be a most unpleasant experience especially if one feels as Sarah did that her opinion was the correct one. In order to prove her point, she chose for the first fashion plate the most frivolous mode of dress she could find. The print, made by the Boston lithographers, Pendleton Brothers, pictured a style of dress and coiffeur that were extreme to the point of ridiculous. "London and Parisian Fashions" showed two elegant young ladies *presumably* dressed in the latest and most fashionable mode. In the upper corners of the print were two "heads" depicting face and back views of an absurdly artificial and intricate hair style. Mincing forward on her dainty slippered feet, one of the mademoiselles was attired in an off-the-shoulder, tightly bodiced full-length gown with balloon sleeves and a billowy skirt embroidered with large lacy ferns. Her demure face peeked out from under a huge halo-shaped bonnet accentuated by round curls of hair pinned on each side of her forehead. Her companion, seen from the back, was seated on a delicate chair almost completely hidden by her voluminous skirt. Her fancy bonnet appeared to be the back view of the one worn by her mincing friend. Little wonder Sarah thought such fashions unfit for the American housewife. Her position was clearly stated. Women should wear clothes that are becoming, graceful, and appropriate regardless of fashion trends and dictates.

Accompanying the Pendleton plate was a comment criticizing the blind way American women followed European styles, some created solely for them because of their gullibility. Sarah hoped the day would come when she could show fashions designed and executed by American women which would reward "a small share of the taste and talent that only wait for the sunshine of public encouragement to burst forth—and beautify the land."

Please think for yourselves, fair readers, was her advice; think for yourselves not only in questioning fashion trends but also in other concerns affecting your lives. This sensible approach caused considerable comment, but it also evoked a great deal of unfavorable criticism.

Although her readers showed a willingness to follow Sarah's advice on many matters, they refused to follow her lead in the realm of fashion. Her books on cooking, manners, social improvement, and family living sold extremely well, and her opinions in these fields were quoted and followed in homes throughout the nation. However, it was not in her power to markedly affect fashion trends or to lessen the tremendous popularity of the fashion prints.

In December 1830 an announcement appeared on Sarah's editorial pages stating that future numbers of the publication would be published by Marsh, Copen and Lyon. The new publishers promised there would be six plates, engravings or lithographs, a year.

Sarah was still writing poems for the magazine but less fiction, spending more time on independent projects of her own. She was busy gathering botanical information and short poems or individual verses for her gift book *Flora's Interpreter* to be published in 1832. The other activities claiming her attention were many and varied. Her literary club was in full swing, and at least one afternoon a month she met with a group of Beacon Hill women to sew for the needy seamen and their families. This sewing circle was the unpretentious beginning of the Seamen's Aid Society of Boston. Sarah also attended many lectures and reported on some in her magazine.

One woman who became a fairly regular contributor to the magazine was Elizabeth Oakes Smith. She wrote from Portland, Maine, asking Sarah's advice about getting started on a writing career, and this was the beginning of a long friendship between the two women. Years later their affection for one another would come under considerable strain because they would not see eye to eye on the question of the propriety of women lecturing in public, but in the mid-thirties Sarah was the considerate teacher and Elizabeth her very apt pupil.

6   Pioneer
in Education

"The education of women," said Jean-Jacques Rousseau, "should always be relative to men. To please, to be useful to us, to make us love and esteem them, to educate when young and to take care of us when grown up, to advise us, to console us, to render our lives easy and agreeable; these are the duties of women at all times." This concept had a surprising number of advocates in the eighteen hundreds; but fortunately for future generations of women, there were also some intelligent educationists in America who wholeheartedly disagreed with Rousseau's theory. Sarah aligned herself with men and women who were leaders in an educational movement to improve conditions for women so that they would have an opportunity to develop their mental powers and to become more knowledgeable members of society. Some of these dedicated people were Catherine Beecher, Mary Lyons, Catherine Fiske, John Blake, William Woodbridge, Elizabeth Peabody, and Almira Phelps and her more illustrious sister Emma Willard.

In 1828 there were not many schools for girls, and only a few offered more than "a limited amount of literature, a little edifying history, devotional and moral reading, and such ornaments as music, sketching and dancing." Sarah wanted to see seminaries established that would teach a wider range of subjects and more advanced courses of study, that would train teachers and then send out young women to found more schools. She told her readers that their editor's "favorite subject" was the sponsorship of women in the teaching profession. She had not then begun her fight for better working conditions and *higher wages* for women, or she might have worded her plea for the acceptance of women as teachers in a different manner. Women not only make excellent teachers, she said, but they are willing to work for less money and "to make education universal, it must be made cheap." Closely linked with this favorite subject was the promotion of better and more schools for girls, a first step before they could become qualified teachers.

Sarah had a personal interest in this project, for Frances and Josepha were attending the Young Ladies Seminary in Keene not far from the home of their Uncle Selma. This school was founded by Catherine Fiske in 1814 and held the distinction of being the oldest of its kind in the nation. On a trip to see the girls Sarah visited the school and was impressed with its excellent standards. She had started a series on existing schools for girls, and Keene Seminary was discussed in this department and given a high recommendation. For the series she had the advice and backing of her friend John Blake. The catalog of the school being described was usually her source of information, and Sarah quoted freely from this in order to acquaint interested parents with the method of application, the curriculum, and the costs and arrangements for boarding students. Also included was a brief history of the school.

In 1828 the Infant School Society of Boston was founded to promote the establishment of schools for the children of poor working mothers. The children, between eighteen-months and four-years-old, were too young to attend other schools. In publicizing the good work of the Society in February of 1829, Sarah wrote a long editorial stressing the importance of training for little children in preparation for entering the larger more disciplined classrooms they would enter later. Then she suggested that children other than the poor could benefit by the formation of similar infant schools, then a novel idea.

Sarah had already begun a department in her magazine on child psychology called "Letters from a Mother." Some of the letters were actually from mothers; however, most were written by the editor to get her point across. The advice was based on common sense and Sarah's experience as a mother and a teacher. Although the advice in some of the letters has an old-fashioned ring, much has stood the test of time. Some of her suggestions seemed such a sharp breakaway from established Puritan concepts that they caused raised eyebrows and even controversy; but many mothers who eagerly awaited the next month's "Letter" quoted her advice and "But Mrs. Hale says—"was soon heard throughout the country. This column became so popular that it was continued for a number of years, and its effect plus editorials on infant schools had the desired results. Other schools were started, one as early as September of that first year, 1828.

Another project in Sarah's busy schedule came about because of her friendship with the composer Lowell Mason, a man who shared her interest in child psychology. As a result of an increased awareness of music by the general public, Sarah had started including a piece of sheet music in each *Ladies' Magazine,* and this awareness also lay behind a proposal Lowell Mason made to her. He had a theory that school children could learn about the world around them by singing suitable verses set to music, and he asked Sarah to write some poems for this use. One result of his request was a paperback book of fifteen poems called *Poems for Our Children*, published in 1830 by Marsh, Capen and Lyon. The little book included the celebrated poem "Mary's Lamb" and another one which was almost as popular at that time, a paraphrase of the Lord's Prayer.

> Our Father in heaven
>   We hallow thy name!
> May thy kingdom be holy,
>   On earth be the same—
> O, give to us daily,
>   Our portion of bread!
> It is from thy bounty
>   That all must be fed.
>
> Forgive our transgressions,
>   And teach us to know
> The humble compassion
>   That pardons each foe—
> Keep us from temptation,
>   From weakness and sin—
> And thine shall be glory
>   Forever—Amen!

In all of the poems the words and rhymes were simple, and each contained a moral lesson. Eight of these verses of Sarah's were included in Lowell Mason's popular song book, the *Juvenile Lyre*, which spread throughout New England and was the beginning of musical education in schools. Lowell Mason had brought the sound of music into the classroom, and children skipped home singing the little verses written by Sarah.

Of much interest to Sarah was the progress being made by Dr. Samuel Howe in teaching the blind. Horatio had entered the Chauncey School in Cambridge where he was studying in preparation for Harvard College. Dr. Howe was one of his professors at the school and became interested in Horatio because of his outstanding scholastic ability. When the doctor learned that the boy's mother was a widow struggling to support and educate a family, he offered to give some financial backing for his future education. In this way Sarah came to know Dr. Howe both as a friend and benefactor.

In 1831 Samuel Howe took over the management of the Boston school for the blind which later became the famed Perkins Institution. Under forty years of his extremely capable administration, the school attained the reputation of the leading school for the blind in the world, a reputation it still holds. Dr. Howe took Sarah through the school in 1832, and she was greatly impressed with how well the pupils managed in a number of subjects: reading, geography, mathematics, work shop, and especially music. They were given both vocal and instrumental instruction. The doctor wanted to make his students feel they were a part of the school-going public, and he also wished them trained to be self-supporting. Accordingly broom making and piano tuning were included in the curriculum.

In the January 1833 *Ladies' Magazine*, Sarah wrote about her visit to the school, reviewed Dr. Howe's pioneer work and told her readers how successful his methods were and how amazingly well the students were progressing in their studies. Some of her Boston women friends held fairs to benefit the institution. In March, when Sarah spoke about the fairs, she asked women from other communities to follow their lead. This effort was one that Sarah publicized and promoted for many years.

Another pioneer in the field of education who received

Sarah's enthusiastic support was Emma Willard. Emma Hart Willard was only a year and a half older than Sarah and their backgrounds ran along parallel lines beginning with their Connecticut ancestry. Emma was a direct descendant of Thomas Hooker, the founder of Hartford. Both Sarah and Emma, as girls, had been frustrated by the lack of formal education available for women, although Emma did have some formal schooling; both started teaching while still in their teens and continued to take an active part in promoting better educational opportunities for girls. They were also fortunate to marry men who staunchly supported them in their interests.

Emma objected strongly to Rousseau's definition of the proper education for women, and she determined to prove how grossly unfair it was to her sex by showing how capable women can be if given the tools of eduation. In her opinion "Education should seek to bring its subjects to the perfection of their moral, intellectual and physical nature, in order that they may be of the greatest possible use to themselves and others; or, to use a different expression, that they may be the means of the greatest happiness of which they are capable, both as to what they enjoy and what they communicate."

In 1819, when Sarah was still a contented wife and mother living in Newport, Emma had petitioned the New York state legislature for financial assistance in establishing a quality school for young women. The presentation she made received national recognition because it was so well thought out and written. Approval of the plan came from important men like President Monroe, Thomas Jefferson, and many members of Congress; John Adams wrote her a long flattering letter. Yet no state aid was forthcoming!

The city of Troy, New York, was an "up-and-coming" community, and citizens there became interested in the revolutionary plan for a girls' school which would be the most advanced in the country. They offered Emma financial backing if the school were established in their city, and the Troy Female Seminary was founded in 1821.

Emma had lived for a number of years in Vermont directly across from Middlebury College and had had an excellent oppportunity to learn about the courses being studied by young men. She modeled her seminary courses somewhat on those given at Middlebury; however, one concession was made when physiology was introduced into the curriculum. To preserve the modesty of the girls and to avoid criticism by their parents, heavy paper was pasted over the pages of the textbooks depicting the human body.

The Troy Seminary was one of the earliest, if not the first, of the normal schools for girls. Emma's main intent was to train teachers and then encourage them to start schools in other localities, a most successful endeavor. When Catherine Beecher wrote from Cincinnati that thousands of teachers were needed on the rapidly expanding western frontier, Emma responded by sending a number of her graduates out West. Other proteges returned to their home states and established schools there.

Four years after the founding of the Troy Seminary, Emma's husband died leaving her with the entire responsibility for running the school. She missed his companionship and felt lost without his behind-the-scenes business management, and yet she carried on without his help. Her only child, other than stepchildren, was a fifteen-year-old son John. His mother secured an appointment for him at West Point. John was senior there the year David Hale was a freshman, and their mothers met at the Academy in 1829. Although Sarah had known the educator through her work, she had not been acquainted with her until they met at West Point.

The two women, friends from the first, formed stronger ties in 1833 while cooperating on a project. Like many thoughtful people they had rejoiced when Greece gained her independence from Turkey. Many Americans sought ways to help the Greek nation regain some of the cultural attributes lost during the decline of her civilization. Emma Willard hoped to assist by establishing a normal school similar to her seminary, and so she founded a society in Troy for this purpose and wrote articles to advance this cause. Sarah published one of her articles "Advancement of Female Education," in the *Book*. By this time the magazine was circulated in every state in the Union. Scarcely an issue appeared in 1833 without some mention of Emma's fund raising project.

Many of Emma's graduates raised money in their own localities, and Sarah's friend Lydia Sigourney headed a fund-raising drive in Hartford. When the mission was successful, three women were delighted that a normal school would soon be established in Athens—three women who had become close friends while working for this cause: Emma Willard, Lydia Sigourney, and Sarah Hale. From that year on, Emma and Sarah often visited the Sigourneys in Hartford, and the women kept in touch by corresponding frequently.

7 Bunker Hill Monument

Women succeed where men had failed? Women raise enough money for the completion of the Bunker Hill Monument when thousands of dollars would be required? How could any woman in her right mind make so preposterous a proposition? And where were the ladies to acquire the money? Steal from their husbands? The press was up in arms.

Sarah had anticipated some unfavorable reaction when she made her offer to the Monument Association in January of 1830, but nothing as satirical and scathing as the editorials which appeared in the Boston newspapers. The Monument Association members, hesitant at first, had voted to "gratefully" accept her suggestion that the requisite money might be raised by an appeal to the women of New England. If they were willing, why should the press be so antagonistic?

"The press" at that time was almost totally male-dominated. Sarah was an exception; few women had her opportunity to influence the thinking public. What would the effects of this influence be? Was a woman trying to tell men how to handle their money? Or worse still, was her purpose to pursuade the ladies to enter into *all* the affairs of men? Would male prerogatives be chipped away piece by piece? Sarah's suggestion seemed to indicate a dangerous trend, at least so thought some newspaper men.

One particularly sarcastic and deprecatory comment by Joseph Buckingham in the *Commercial Gazette* especially hurt Sarah, for she admired the *Gazette* editor and had considered him to be her friend. Finding bigotry in otherwise intelligent individuals is always depressing. Buckingham's editorials and other press releases were extremely discouraging. All she wished to do was help a worthwhile project to be a success, nothing more, and so Sarah refused to be intimidated.

The unfinished monument was a constant and bleak reminder of a grand dream that appeared to be doomed and never be a reality. The four-sided, forty-foot pillar with its jagged unfinished top rising from a huge platform with tons of granite blocks strewn around the base was a bedraggled sight. The tower was missing one hundred and eighty feet of its proposed height plus the pyramid point that would transform the monstrosity into a slender obelisk, an historic shrine to commemorate the Battle of Bunker Hill fought on the spot on June 17, 1775.

What had become of all the enthusiasm generated five years earlier on the occasion of the fiftieth anniversary of the battle when the cornerstone of the monument was laid? Thousands of cheering, flag-waving spectators had walked along beside the long parade of soldiers and dignitaries, stirred by the music of marching bands, all the way from the Boston Common to the summit of the Hill. What had become of all the patriotic fervor aroused by Webster when he made his impassioned dedicatory address? The success of the mission appeared to be assured with so many people so deeply moved; however, most of those members of the celebration throng did little of a financial nature to aid the monument's construction. No person there that day dreamed the work would drag on year after year nor did any have any notion of the expense of completion. Certainly the dedicated and public-spirited men who had agreed to serve as members of the Monument Association and oversee the financing and construction did not realize how many problems they were to encounter. Now five years and fifty thousand dollars later, the association had run out of funds and more money did not appear to be forthcoming. When Sarah made her proposal of aid, these men were ready to grab at any straw; yes, even to the extent of accepting help from a woman.

The first action she took was to print in the February issue of the *Ladies' Magazine* an editorial about the sorry plight of the monument project and then to request a one-dollar donation from each subscriber, the first such solicitation ever made in a periodical. Sarah pointed out at the same time that the construction would provide work for many Boston men who badly needed jobs. It was the request for donations from the women that had alarmed some members of the press.

The following month after a thank-you message to all the readers who had supported her over the years, Sarah said that they appeared to be behind her one hundred percent in her effort to see the monument completed. She had hoped for cooperation from all the Boston editors as well, but a few refused their support. Yet she felt justified in proceeding although "we would by no means recommend to any lady to join the Society without the consent of her immediate protector," the holder of the purse strings. Then with further placation she explained that the women were offering assistance with no intent to degrade the men.

A Committee of Correspondence made up of wealthy and influential Boston women began immediately writing letters to women across New England explaining their mission and asking for donations. Sarah asked other communities to form committees to raise funds.

Month after month Sarah urged readers to join the ranks of interested citizens by contributing to the monument fund. She also composed stories and verse aimed at arousing patriotic ardor and one poem, "The Last of the Band," was particularly successful in swelling the fund. Unfortunately, all her zeal and the effort of other women did not bring in sufficient money to further the construction, a huge disappointment for Sarah and her co-workers.

By September the fund totaled just under three thousand dollars, far short of the fifty thousand needed to finish the monument. With heavy heart Sarah informed her readers about the situation. Defeat was hard to swallow, especially after the ridicule of their endeavor by the press. The money collected, said the editor in the *Ladies' Magazine*, had been invested in the Massachusetts Hospital Insurance Company in a separate account "to be denominated the Ladies' Fund until larger sums become available." Much of the fund-raising problem had its roots in the novelty of requesting financial assistance from women rather than men; however, this was not the complete answer. The young country's finances were shaky and people were beginning to feel the pinch of an oncoming depression. The Bunker Hill Monument would have to remain unfinished for the time being.

Four years later the Monument Association requested the assistance of the Boston Mechanic Association and received almost twenty thousand dollars. To this sum was added the Ladies' Fund of three thousand and the tower was raised another eighty feet before the money ran out again. One hundred and twenty feet had taken nine years and close to seventy-three thousand dollars to construct and there was still another one hundred feet to go! Six years went by with no change in the situation.

During this six-year period Sarah's reputation as a thoughtful, highly motivated and competent editor had grown, and her influence had spread into more and more homes across the country with a far wider circulation of the *Ladies' Magazine*. In Boston her list of acquaintances was not limited to the intellectually and socially elite but extended to people in all walks of life through her action in welfare projects. When another opportunity to aid the Bunker Hill Monument came along, she was ready for the challenge.

At a meeting in the home of one of her Beacon Hill friends, a meeting in connection with the women's effort to improve the living conditions of needy seamen and their families, Sarah first heard of a sad prognosis made by the Monument Association members in their June 1840 Annual Report. The doubt was raised "whether the present generation will have the pleasure to see the monument completion." The women were shocked by this statement that reflected utter discouragement on the part of the club members. Many women present had served ten years earlier on the Committee of Correspondence during the first drive for funds. Could they do more now? The first experience had shown that it was impossible to raise large sums of money from women whose family finances were mainly controlled by the husband-head or father-head of the household. So, what could the ladies do to make money? They could sew and they could cook. Recent fairs held for charitable causes had proved successful. Why not hold a fair on a much larger scale, one which would include contributions from the women of New England and even more distant communities rather than from just those in Boston? When this idea was presented to the Monument Association, the members voted to accept this offer of further assistance from the ladies.

Just eight days after the vote was passed by the men, preparations for the big fair were underway. Hundreds of letters sped from Boston to all parts of the nation. Newspapers throughout New England were asked to publicize the fair and to request donations. Knitting and crochet kneedles clicked as far west as Ohio and south into Maryland and the Carolinas as patriotic women joined with New Englanders in projects to benefit the fund-raising drive. Some women preserved jellies, jams, and pickles while others started patchwork quilts or began working on fancy embroidery. Transporting all the products to Boston must have been quite an undertaking. Perishable items like fresh-baked pies, cakes, cookies, rolls, and bread were brought in just before or on opening day.

Quincy Hall was the place chosen for the mammoth fair because it was the largest suitable building in Boston. The ring of excited voices and the clatter of noisy feet filled the hall the week before the big event as decisions were made about the placement of tables, the display of goods, and the arrangement of decorations. Pricing the wares was difficult and time-consuming; Sarah insisted that all the items for sale be new and that they be fairly marked according to commercial value, not hiked up just to bring in more money. Then in a pep talk to her volunteer saleswomen, she suggested that the women smile, act graciously, and be exceedingly pleasant so that customers might *want* to pay more for their purchases than the goods were worth.

On September fifteenth the doors of Quincy Hall were thrown open for the start of the fair—less than three months after the Monument Association members' unhappy prediction. Thousands flocked to the Fair, more than four thousand on opening day alone. The roads leading into the city must have been packed with carriages, gigs, wagons, people on foot, and others on horseback. Where were they able to "park" all the horse drawn vehicles? Every hitching post within a one-mile radius of Quincy Hall must have been taxed to the limit. Others came by boat and walked up to the Hall from the wharves.

During the six days of record crowds and record sales, Sarah edited a small daily newspaper, the *Monument*, giving a running account of the progress of the fair. Some of the articles for sale were given a plug, items ranging all the way from two fancy cakes to a piano. She edited the paper on the spot; it sold for six and a half cents, and proceeds from its sale netted five hundred and fifty-six dollars for the fair. Along with the sales pitch and her own editorials, short poems, and anecdotes were literary contributions from some of her friends; for example, Hannah Gould, Lydia Sigourney, and Elizabeth Oakes Smith. Sarah also included a list of people who made money donations. Mr. Lawrence of the Mechanic Association very generously gave twenty thousand dollars, and ten thousand came from a man in New Orleans who was a former Boston resident, with others giving lesser amounts. The *Monument* reported the gift of "a single lady," a French ballerina named Fanny Ellsler—the superb dancer who made her Boston debut the same week the fair was in progress.

The money-raising event lasted only a week, but in that short space of time the women made thirty thousand dollars in addition to the money contributions. The total was sufficient to finish the construction of the Bunker Hill column according to the original plans. The pride (and relief) experienced by the Monument Association members was great, and the men did not hesitate to give some of the credit to Sarah and all the women who had helped the cause so much. "The project was successful beyond expectations," said the 1843 Records of the Association. "Thousands flocked to the scene; and the abundance, variety, and beauty of the articles exhibited, as well as the arrangements, were credible to the highest degree to the industry, taste, skill, and spirit of the Ladies of New England."

On June 17, 1843, eighteen long years after the cornerstone of the monument was laid, there was another Bunker Hill ceremony—this time to mark the final completion of the national shrine. President Tyler was present with members of his cabinet, and there were many soldiers, dignitaries, and spectators. Once more Webster was asked to speak and in his oration he praised all the gallant men who had fought on the Hill in "the first great battle of the Revolution," soldiers who not only struck the "first blow" for the independence of their country but also "the blow which determined the contest." The eloquent orator declared that "When the sun of that day went down, the event of independence was certain."

Sarah was a proud spectator that day on the Hill. As she listened to Webster's speech, perhaps she was thinking about another "first blow" that the monument completion represented—a blow struck in a battle fought by the women of America under her leadership. Their fight had broken a link in the chain of prejudice which had always kept women behind the scenes in matters requiring social action. Surely, never again would the male element of our society take so lightly the act of women uniting in order to fight in behalf of a worthwhile cause. The Bunker Hill Monument honors brave men who took a stand for the independence of their young country, but it also commemorates brave women who took a stand for the independence of their sex.

8 Seamen's Aid Society

The only woman's organization in the nation before the completion of the Bunker Hill Monument was the Seamen's Aid Society of Boston founded by Sarah in 1833. She became the first president, a board member, keeper of the official records, and its guiding light until her departure for Philadelphia in 1841. The purpose of the Seamen's Aid Society was to alleviate the dire living conditions of sailors and their families in the large port city. In this effort the women joined forces with the Boston Port Society established by the Reverend Edward T. Taylor, the clergyman so greatly admired by Longfellow. Taylor preached to the sailors at the Seaman's Church in Boston's North Square and also worked with his organization to improve the lot of the sailor.

The sea-related industries of fishing and shipping were second in importance only to agriculture in our country's economy. Historians paint in glowing colors the spectacular water front of Boston, the busiest harbor in the United States at that time. "The pride of the city," said William Rossiter, "was its water front stretching from north to south, indented and built up with spacious docks and wharves, with a forest of masts and spars, and a wealth of snowy canvas such as no other city in the Union could boast—so far as the extent and variety of its commerce was concerned" Boston had no equal in the country. "There was no quarter of the civilized globe in which the enterprise, energy, and pluck of a Boston shipmaster did not find entrance, or from which a wealth of commerce did not return."

The captains of these sailing vessels and the merchants prospered, but what about the sailors who manned the ships sailing to foreign ports? And what about the families they left behind? In spite of the hazardous job of the seaman, he was at the bottom of the wage scale. The most he could hope to earn was eighteen dollars a week, and he often made as little as ten. From this scant sum a man had to outfit himself, which sometimes meant having to ask for an advance of two-months pay. When the married sailor took to sea, he frequently left behind a family ill clothed and with not enough money to buy necessities. His wife was forced to work, and job opportunities were limited. She could take in washing or work for the owner of a clothing store which outfitted seamen. If she had small children, the woman sometimes did piece work at home. The wages paid to these women were so miserly that the most industrious seamstress working long hours could only hope to earn from sixty cents to a dollar a week! Then this clothing was sold to the sailor at inflated prices because the store operator had to give a kickback to the keeper of the boarding house who sent sailors to his shop. The families of the common sailors constituted one of the major poverty problems in our country.

Sarah had never before seen the ravages of industrial poverty, and its grimness appalled her. The first remedial action she took against the injustice was the formation of the Seamen's Aid Society in January of 1833. When she also became president of the woman's organization that month, she was on the threshold of a year crowded with work and activities, a busy year that also brought about three changes in her personal life.

Her brother Horatio died at age forty-seven and Sarah felt his loss keenly. In July, David graduated from West Point, the youngest in a class of one hundred and fifty cadets but thirteenth in honor rank. The day he was commissioned Brevet Second Lieutenant was a proud one for his mother. The following month young Horatio entered Harvard as a boarding student, choosing linguistics for his major. Both girls were attending Emma Willard's Seminary in Troy.

The following January, 1834, the *Ladies' Magazine* became the *American Ladies' Magazine*. Sarah told her readers that "we found there was a British periodical called the 'Ladies' Magazine'. We wished to have ours distinguished as American."

The Seamen's Aid Society did not receive the publicity given to the Bunker Hill Monument. The editor realized that the majority of her readers would have little interest in the plight of sailors in Boston. And so without the backing of her magazine, Sarah began the welfare project which proved to be the most successful one of her entire career.

The early activities of the Seaman's Aid were very modest indeed, little more that a sewing circle of well-intentioned Boston society women who met once a week to make clothes for sailors and their families. The women spent the afternoon "making garments to be given to the poor" Sarah wrote in her 1836 Annual Report "when the greatest need for most of them was—employment." In this approach to social welfare Sarah was almost a hundred years ahead of her times. She advocated providing jobs with adequate and prompt payment rather than outright charity which she felt would make the poor dependent paupers and also foster crime.

The women put their heads together and came up with an excellent idea. They would open a clothing store and employ the sailors' wives to make outfits for the men. The working conditions would be far superior and the wives would receive higher wages. But this would require money. The Society held a fair which realized a thousand dollars. From this sum three hundred was used to open the store which the ladies furnished by digging into their attics. Opening day was February 26, 1834 and the store was an instant success. Sarah reported that the society members had to make a "delicate" decision in determining how much to pay the seamstresses, for they wanted each worker to earn enough for self support and yet be able to sell the clothing to the seamen at reasonable prices. Three dollars a week was set as a fair wage. During the last ten months of the first year of operation, the store netted over two thousand dollars and paid wages to fifty women. In spite of the fact that the garments sold at lower rates than were charged by the slop shops, the women made enough profit to enable them to start other branches of their charitable movement—much to the great indignation of the men who had been fleecing the sailors for years.

The owners of the clothing stores and boarding houses were up in arms. They could see the do-gooders robbing them of all their profits and a battle ensued. Sarah was ready for the challenge. She wrote that the owners of the lodging houses were despicable, as low as the miserable dives they operated. They were dispensers of filthy rooms, unwholesome food, and miserable grog. And the store owners were no better. They expected the women to work for a pittance under unhealthy conditions.

Sarah described some of the violent clashes between the store owners and the members of the Society in her 1834 Annual Report. The protesting owners lost the battle, especially the boarding house keepers. The President of the Seamen's Aid Society suggested that the organization establish its own lodging house for sailors—to be operated at cost. The one the women founded was called "Mariner's House." When Sarah made an appeal for furnishings for the new home, she predicted that "Immense will be the blessings and benefits these Society boarding houses will confer." From this start sprang all the Seaman's Hostels, Snug Harbors, and Sailors' Homes which helped seafaring men and their families.

The Society took the entire family of the seamen into consideration. A trade school for girls was founded where they were taught cutting, fitting, and sewing by expert tailors. The girls were also given courses in domestic science, a term coined by Sarah to give housework the dignity of a profession. A direct result of these trade schools was the establishment of a Social Library. At first only the girls were permitted to borrow books, but soon this privilege was extended to all members of the family. News of the library spread along the eastern seacoast from Maine to Florida, and many communities asked the society for second-hand books and periodicals. In time lighthouse keepers and the coast guard became beneficiaries of this unique service which grew into the present day Merchant Marine Library Association.

Sarah's projects in behalf of seamen and their families met with such phenomenal success that she was totally unprepared for two successive failures, failures which occurred because the measures she proposed were too advanced for the times. One project was an offshoot of the Mariner's House. The married sailors had housing problems, too; they were being charged excessively high rents for inferior dwellings. When Sarah pointed out that "Very few tenements have been contructed with reference to the wants of the poor" and advocated the erection of "model tenements," she was so far ahead of her era that the suggestion fell on deaf ears. When she spoke about "the effect of environment on character," many people did not have the least notion what she meant. Her better housing for the poor was a complete failure.

Her second defeat came when she campaigned for the retention of property rights for married women. In 1836 a sad situation had come to her attention. A woman who worked at the Store ran into problems in the middle of winter while her husband was away at sea. This woman had managed for the first time in her married life to give her children some of life's comforts because of her earnings at the Store. Then one of her husband's creditors sized up the situation and her earnings were seized to pay the man. She was not the first sailor's wife to have her income confiscated because of debts incurred by the head of the family. Other people found out about the improved financial status provided by the Store and were quick to collect their debts. Sarah, the society, and the sailors' wives were helpless to prevent this practice because the law stated that once a woman married all she owned belonged to her husband.

At the end of 1836 the *American Ladies' Magazine* merged with Godey's *Lady's Book* and Sarah became the literary editor of the combined publication. In May of 1837 she wrote an editorial in the *Lady's Book* addressed to the state legislature on the subject of "The Rights of Married Women." The editor was most reluctant to abandon a cause she felt so strongly about. In the article Sarah presented her views on the issue clearly and emphatically saying that there should be no place in a Christian community for "The barbarous custom of wresting from woman whatever she possesses, whether by inheritance, donation or by her own industry, and conferring it all upon the man she marries, to be used at his discretion and will, perhaps wasted on his wicked indulgences, without allowing her any control or redress... ." Fighting the law of the land was quite a different story from combating the injustices of the landlords of boarding houses and the owners of the slop shops, and Sarah got nowhere in her battle.

Although the two lost causes were a bitter disappointment, Sarah's social welfare action on behalf of the seamen had accomplished a great deal, much of lasting value: the havens for sailors, the trade schools, and the social library which was the cornerstone of the Merchant Marine Library. The lot of seafaring men and their families was considerably improved by all the effort of the Seamen's Aid Society, and this first organization of American women is also credited with being the first to promote better working conditions and higher wages for women—and the first to *begin* the fight for the retention of property rights for married women.

9   Louis Godey
and
Lady's Book

Despite the depression of 1836 resulting from the banking problems in President Jackson's administration, Sarah's career changed for the better, linking her business destiny with that of the publisher Louis Godey. These two, so strikingly different in personality, shared an active interest in the emergence of the nineteenth-century woman and a sincere wish to cater to her growing needs and ever-widening range of interests. The spectacular success of their joint effort owed much to the genius of Louis Godey.

Louis Antoine Godey was born in New York City on June 6, 1804. His parents, Louis and Margaret Godey, had fled from France during the French Revolution. They were not well-to-do and their son was mainly self-educated. He received some of his printing experience working for city newspapers. Louis had a great love of books, and with the first money he managed to save he opened a small combination news stand and book store which he operated for several years. In 1828, the year Sarah left her New Hampshire home town for Boston, Louis Godey went to Philadelphia to become a "scissors editor" in the composing room of the *Daily Chronicle*. He soon graduated to office work where he learned about the administrative side of the publishing business in preparation for what was to become his life's work.

In 1830 Godey entered the publishing field with the first edition of his magazine for women, the *Lady's Book*. He was a shrewd businessman, a master showman with an innate ability to sense what would please his public, and a flair for publicity that made it possible for him to capitalize to the fullest on his instincts. A complete extrovert, Louis Godey was endowed with qualities that were to see him through some very lean years, an abundance of energy and enthusiasm, and, most important of all, tremendous self confidence.

In appearance and attributes other than his business acumen, Godey so exactly resembled Dickens's Mr. Pickwick that it is hard to believe that Dickens met Louis *after* he had created his character. Like Pickwick, he was "Rotund, urbane, ingratiating, susceptible to flattery and impervious to criticism, endowed with an unshakeable faith in his own observations and withal devoted to the 'fair ladies.' "

Godey was not the only Philadelphia publisher trying for success on a shoe string and having his troubles compounded by the financial problems of the early 1830s. T. S. Arthur wrote a story supposedly based on the early career of Mr. Godey. In the story "Anything Over Today," Mr. Arthur told about a system that was used by many businessmen in the city at that time. Their affairs were operated on such a close margin that there was always one man who was lacking funds when a note came due. The current practice was to make the rounds of other firms looking for someone who had enough "over" for the day to be in a position to lend money to his hard-pressed friend. More than once young Godey was saved from financial ruin by this lend-a-hand system.

The *Lady's Book* was a second-rate magazine during the six and a half years before Sarah became its literary editor. Under Godey's management the periodical contained mainly reprints from English works with infrequent pieces snipped from American newspapers and a rare article or story marked "written expressly for the *Lady's Book*." There were a few household hints, cooking recipes, and articles on embroidery but no book reviews or informational articles to stimulate the intellect of his readers. The sole purpose of the *Lady's Book* was to entertain "the fair ladies" for whom he had a high regard.

At the back of the magazine were a few pages reserved by the publisher for comments which in time came to be called the "Arm Chair." Here the gallant Mr. Godey flattered his "dear readers" by taking the ladies into his confidence and talking with them about his problems and successes. Every favorable mention or review of the *Lady's Book* printed in other periodicals appeared on these pages. The "Arm Chair" chats brought the congenial Mr. Godey many devoted readers.

When Godey first started referring to his magazine as the *Book*, a great number of people thought he was being sacrilegious. The only book with the right to be capitalized was the good *Book* and so the publisher changed the nickname of his magazine to "The Book." Scoffers still derisively spoke of "Godey's Bible" or sometimes even "God-ey's Bible," but "The Book" kept its appellation. In the back of the *Book*, along with the "Arm Chair" department, Godey began the practice of placing advertisements of the local merchants and their wares. This custom has carried over to the present day, and advertisements are still referred to as being "in the back of the book."

One costly and extremely frustrating problem that frequently came up for discussion in the "Arm Chair" department in the thirties was the trouble caused by the complete unreliability of the United States mail service. The railroads were so new that most of the mail was carried either by stage coach or steamboat. Month after month the publisher had to apologize for magazines which arrived late or worse still—not at all. In a February issue one such apology stated

> Our subscribers, during this season of the year, must have a little patience with us. Our work is always ready on time, but we cannot control the elements .... December numbers for our Eastern agents were shipped early in December. Where the vessel got to with them, we are unable to say, but they did not arrive in Boston until a few days before the January number .... A bundle was returned to us from the Post Office containing a lot of December numbers reduced to a jelly, and looking like the material in a paper-maker's vat, absolutely reduced to first principles .... We very much fear our February number will be late coming to hand, as the roads are in dreadful condition.

Godey did his best to compensate for the deficiencies of the mail service by promising each subscriber a replacement copy for any magazine that failed to arrive at its proper destination, a promise which cut into his profits. Many struggling publishers had their businesses ruined because of mailing problems. Others settled for local customers only; however, Godey was fighting for a national circulation and was determined to achieve his goal. One advantage to businessmen was the method employed at that time for paying mailing costs: the receiver, not the sender, paid the postage, and this practice may have been the saving grace for Louis Godey.

The first edition of the *Lady's Book* and all subsequent ones contained a colored fashion print. These early engravings were purchased at a reduced rate from the Philadelphia publishing house of Hart and Carey. Mathew Carey knew both Godey and Sarah, and he may have been instrumental in getting the future partners acquainted.

As early as 1834 Sarah had begun to feel the pinch of hard times. Her magazine subscriptions had fallen off sharply and many reliable customers had started to neglect paying their accounts. Hoping to change the discouraging trend, she made an appeal to her subscribers asking them to please come to her assistance. By this time she had become part owner of her magazine.

That same year Godey did not appear to be suffering from financial difficulties—quite the contrary. For the first time he was making a real effort to secure some original articles and stories for his *Book*. He printed nine original contributions in January 1835. That the publisher was willing to pay for material rather than just reprint the works of others was indicative of a more firm financial footing.

By July Sarah was beginning to feel the full brunt of the depression and she had started dunning subscribers for nonpayment. She told her readers in November that unpaid accounts for 1835 totaled four hundred dollars. She had already been approached by Godey with his request for her services; however, Sarah hoped to hold on to her own magazine. There was also a reason why she did not want to move to Philadelphia; William was about to enter Harvard and his mother wished to remain in Boston till after his graduation. Her answer to Louis Godey was in the negative.

In 1836 David Hale was in Florida fighting in the Seminole War, and Horatio was doing exceptionally well at Harvard. Sarah took pride and personal satisfaction in his writing ability. As early as his freshman year he had many articles printed in the *Harvardianna*, and in his senior year he was one of the three editors of the school magazine. He also took part in the Order of Performance for Exhibition on July 13, 1836.

That same month Godey branched out in the publishing field by starting a weekly newspaper, the *Saturday News*, with two partners, Joseph Neal and Morton McMichael. This additional work load made it imperative for him to have editorial assistance with his magazine. He could have asked one of the well-qualified men he knew, but he felt a woman would be better suited for the position—and he had the perfect answer to his needs in Sarah Josepha Hale.

Some writers have claimed that flattery was the tool he employed to convince Sarah to accept the position. True, he did compliment her and gave favorable notices of her books and also published a long poem written by Horatio—an action bound to please a proud mother. All this no doubt had a softening effect; however, three other factors figured more prominently in the decision making. The depression with its adverse results was a primary cause. Then Godey offered to buy her magazine and merge it with the *Lady's Book*. When he also agreed to let Sarah edit the combined periodical from Boston, all her reservations were broken down. And so in December of 1836, the editor of the *Ladies' Magazine* informed her public that "The first of January will commence a new volume of the *Lady's Book* with which our magazine will be united. We shall take charge of the editorial department."

In that final edition of the *American Ladies' Magazine*, Sarah also stated that the purpose of her magazine during its nine-year life span had been "the advancement of women." She had hoped to continue her periodical, but financial pressures had become too difficult to surmount. Then she assured her readers that the new magazine would be of "a very superior quality." The *Lady's Book* had already shown some encouraging indications of a change of policy for the better with more emphasis on original works by American authors. Godey had announced in September that "with a view to securing *original contributions*" for his *Book*, he would pay "the highest rates for remuneration offered by any periodical in this country."

At the same time that Sarah was explaining the change from *her* magazine to the editorship of the combined periodical, Louis Godey was enthusiastically telling *Lady's Book* readers about the new editor. In the December 1836 issue they learned that

> The present number of the *Lady's Book* closes our career as sole editor. The increasing patronage of the work requires more of our attention in the business department. We are confident our readers will not regret the change, when they learn that Mrs. Sarah Josepha Hale, late editor of the *American Ladies' Magazine* (which is now amalgamated with the *Lady's Book*), will superintend the literary department of the *Book*. Mrs. Hale is too well known to the public to need eulogy from us. For nine years she has conducted the magazine, which she originated, how! its readers well know.... It will therefore be perceived that a new era in the work has been commenced.

The following year William A. Alcott made an interesting comment about the merger of the two magazines. The smaller periodical lost "its identity, and, like many a 'better half,' assumed the name of a worse one. It is united with the *Lady's Book*, a periodical of much interest; but far less important, in its tendencies on sound literature, morals, and education."

True, the *Ladies' Magazine* was far superior to the *Book* before the merger; however, the combined endeavor of the lady editor and the shrewd publisher resulted in a quality magazine which broke all records for popularity and wide circulation; a magazine of great interest to Victorian readers and equally important for those today who are interested in viewing the progress of women during the nineteenth century.

10   The Merger

The merger of the *American Ladies' Magazine* with Godey's *Lady's Book* brought Sarah face-to-face with her former antipathy, the fashion plate, a problem she had avoided for three years by omitting this objectionable feature once she had become part owner of her magazine. However, in the new business set-up, hers was not the last word, and Louis Godey had no intention of casting to one side his pride and joy, the very popular and profitable fashion prints. He was willing to bow to his literary editor's good judgment in most matters concerning magazine content, and he agreed whole-heartedly with her wish to continue the practice of encouraging American talent, but the fashion illustrations were to remain a regular feature of the periodical.

Sarah spent a great amount of time and thought in consideration of how best to present the fashions before coming up with a satisfactory solution, a way to make the illustrations serve as a positive force for female improvement rather than a deterrent. In the January 1837 number of the new *Book*, she made the following statement: "We shall show, before the year is out, the various economical and intellectual benefits of a just simplicity and elegant refinement in the taste for dress." Then, because she was restricted from demonstrating simple and refined fashions, Sarah went on to say "Our engraving of the 'Fashions'…is not given as a pattern for imitation, but as a study for each reader to examine and decide how far this costume is appropriate to her own figure, face and circumstance. This exercise of individual taste is sadly neglected by our fair countrywomen. We seem willing to adopt almost any and every flippery ornament invented by the French and English milliners.... The refined and elegant women of Paris and London would not wear such things."

Emma Willard had just returned from a trip abroad and she substantiated Sarah's position by reporting that "The French ladies are not in dress what they are supposed in our country to be, finical and dashing; but they really understand the matter, and their taste is chaste and correct." Sarah was pleased to have her opinion backed up by her friend and yet she was still unable to convince many of her readers about how naive they were, how much they were duped by foreign designers.

Emma also echoed Sarah's sentiments about fads in dress in her *Journal* when she told about a "very fine" but sadly misled lady who considered herself to be très chic. "Undoubtedly there are in our country more sins against good taste in the choice and blending of colours in apparel, than in modes. We once remarked a very fine lady, and found, on counting the hues that adorned her, that, from her green kid gloves to the lilac bow on the crown of her sky-blue bonnet, she wore no fewer than fifteen distinct colours—sufficient to make two rainbows and a fraction."

Sarah felt no need to apologize for the literary content planned for the *Lady's Book* and she said the poetry "would not yield in excellence to that of any other periodical in the country," and "we shall enrich our pages with the bright prose creations of imagination and reason." Considerable space was to be reserved for the subject of education for women "and women distinguished in this field, such as Mrs. Willard and Mrs. Phelps, will contribute."

A column called "The Lady's Mentor" would continue Sarah's work in publicizing good schools for girls but be enlarged to include information about books of interest to women. The editor also planned to give reports about the state of education for women in Europe as well.

"This then is the final goal of our purpose," wrote Sarah the crusader, "to carry onward and upward the spirit of moral and intellectual excellence in our sex, till their influence shall bless as well as beautify civil society." These principles would be guarded with scrupulous care. We are always at home. For nine years we have presided over the *American Ladies' Magazine*, never relinquishing the trust for a single number. The sphere of that work was circumscribed by many obstacles which it was beyond our power to surmount. The *Book* has a broader field and better prospects. We intend it shall be worthy its popularity, worthy its readers, worthy our country's literature.

Thus the new Godey's *Lady's Book* was launched, captained by Louis Godey with Sarah as navigator and the course it was to follow would make it the most widely circulated magazine of its era.

"There is no universal agent of civilization that exists but our mothers. Nature has placed our infancy in their hands. To this one acknowledged truth, I have been the first to declare, the necessity of making them, by improved education, capable of fulfilling their mission." Sarah was quoting from a book by Aime-Martin, published in 1837, to emphasize the importance of her pet project. This theme of better educational opportunities for women came in for the lion's share of her editorial emphasis during the last half of the first year in her new position. In July the descriptions of three girls' schools she recommended presented a chance to discuss her favorite subject from three different angles.

Miss Draper's Seminary in Hartford, Connecticut, brought up the question: Are men *alone* qualified to head institutions for young ladies? Definitely not! said Sarah. She took exception with many educators who claimed that women were not sufficiently schooled and trained to serve as principals.

Miss D. is principal—she has four female assistant teachers and three male teachers. The responsibility of all the moral management, the manners, and the literary habits and opinions of the young ladies is, as it should be, imposed by a woman—but this does not preclude the advantages of that thorough and scientific course of study for the pupils, which men are doubtless, in some branches, better qualified than women to superintend.

To back her opinion that women are capable of the position of school principal, the editor quoted from a recent letter she had received from Lydia Sigourney. "Your *Lady's Book* takes just the stand it ought. I thank you for speaking out with such independence as you have done about the 'lordly sex' taking charge of female boarding schools. It never ought to be so. Continue to lift your voice on the right side, and posterity will bless you."

A school with a homey atmosphere headed very ably by a married couple was second on her list. The Sibleys' school, Linden Wood, was in St. Charles, Missouri, and Sarah praised Mr. Sibley "for the noble manner in which he has come forward to assist his wife in raising the standard of female education."

St. Mary's Hall in Burlington, New Jersey, was endowed by the Episcopal church. Sarah said that she would not like to see education for either sex made a sectarian matter; "but while legislatures entirely neglect to provide places for the education of females, and while the moral advancement of society is so materially affected by the mental darkness to which women are consigned," the founding and endowing of private seminaries is of paramount importance.

In August the review of Harriet Martineau's book, *Society in America*, gave Sarah further opportunity to plug education for girls. Although not in complete agreement with all the theories propounded by the author, she thought the book as a whole had sufficient merit to warrant recommending it to her readers. One premise in the book she did wholeheartedly support: If women are to have their station raised, they must be prepared to do the groundwork. In the review she said that this opinion was not originated by the author, proving her point by quoting Dr. Spurzheim's statement in his book *Education*: "I most sincerely wish the advancement of women in every respect. But I think of women what I say of nations. If they are looking for a savior from without, they are not yet fit for emancipation."

"Yes, he is right," said Sarah, "women must do the work, or begin it at least. She must cherish a strong hope of the elevation of her sex.... She must devote her thought to the means of improvement. Education, thorough, practical and systematic education for her whole sex must be her aim." Her aim should be "not to depress man, but to exalt him by exalting her who is and must be his companion."

After giving a brief account of much that had already been accomplished by women in England and America, she stated "The work is begun. 'The Female Seminary' at New Hampton, N. H., is prospering. Episcopalians, Baptist and Congregationalists—all are helping the cause." With their assistance women are forging ahead, however, "we cannot learn, neither can we teach, by a sort of magic peculiar to ourselves; give us the facilities for education enjoyed by the other sex, and we shall at least be able to try what are the capabilities of women."

Sermonizing can be boring, and the editor was well aware of the fact that she had been dwelling at great length on her pet subject. After saying she hoped her readers would not weary of such an important subject, Sarah said with pride, "We certainly have reason to feel gratified with the manner in which our efforts in the cause have been thus far received. From all quarters of our Republic information respecting Female Seminaries, and encouraging letters are sent to us."

Sarah's absorption in this subject so close to her heart would not lessen over the years and from time to time she would give a progress report to her public. Perhaps her most enthusiastic one appeared in November of 1841.

> Within the last fifteen or twenty years, more has been written upon the necessity and advantages of female education, than is to be found in all the literature of the preceding ages, since the world began. And what a change, too, in the tone and style of man's writing on the subject. Instead of mocking ridicule, or bitter satire, on every effort of female genius, every attempt to inspire her sex, generally, with the hope of some higher attainments in learning, and a more respectable station in social life than merely that of a household drudge or pretty trifler, we now find, in almost every new publication, whatever may be its design or character, the education and influence of woman on the destiny of the world considered as important subjects.

11   Last Years in Boston

During the mid-thirties a young doctor moved into "Sarah's" boarding house. Oliver Wendell Holmes was attempting to establish a practice in the city. Sarah had admired Holmes before meeting him; his poem "Old Ironsides" hit a responsive chord because it was the type of patriotic literature she sought to foster. This was the beginning of a lifelong friendship.

During part of the time they lived under the same roof, Holmes was plagued with a dilemma—what should he choose as a profession? He had two loves, medicine and creative writing, and he was torn between the two. Sarah was twenty-one years his senior, and Holmes asked for her advice in solving his problem. She encouraged him to continue with his medical career, yet she did not feel this should rule out an active role as a writer. Years later she reversed her opinion, saying that a poet is remembered by posterity while a doctor is usually forgotten along with his "potions." At that time she wished Holmes would devote himself exclusively to writing.

During those Boston years under the same roof, Dr. Holmes aroused Sarah's interest in some of the medical problems of the times. His influence may have played a part in her encouragement and backing of Elizabeth Blackwell in her fight to become a licensed surgeon, her initiation of the concept of women as medical missionaries, and her courageous championing of Dr. William Morton's use of ether in surgery and obstetrics at the time his cause was being attacked by the press and denounced from the pulpit.

Holmes was only one of the many friends Sarah made during the thirties. Through her magazine, the causes she sponsored and her many projects, she came in contact with all sorts of people from many walks of life. Her vivacity, warm personality, and knowledgeable conversation made her a sought-after house guest, and she thoroughly enjoyed dinner parties followed by an evening at the opera, the ballet, a play, or a lyceum lecture—when her busy schedule allowed. Little wonder that her list of acquaintances grew in leaps and bounds; however, her two closest friends lived out-of-state: Lydia Sigourney in Hartford, Connecticut, and Emma Willard in Troy, New York. Trips made to see Frances and Josepha at Emma's school gave Sarah a chance to visit with these two good friends. On her way to and from Troy, she often stayed overnight with the Sigourneys.

By 1837 Emma Willard, who had been a widow eleven years, was a moderately wealthy woman thanks to a great deal of hard work and her superior talents. The money received from the sale of her textbooks plus the profits from her school had put her on a firm financial footing, making her appear very desirable to a certain man who was looking for a well-to-do wife, Dr. Christopher Yates. During his courtship, while the wily doctor spoke of love and devotion, his thoughts were on the money that would become his after the marriage.

It was only after her acceptance of his marriage proposal that Emma began to hear disquieting rumors about her fiance's integrity, that he gambled, that he was a fortune hunter, and that he had been involved in a law suit of some sort.

News filtered through the grapevine can vary from cold facts, to half-truths and even pure fabrication; but the grapevine is sometimes a warning system and as such should not be entirely discounted. When she tried to check on the veracity of the rumors, Emma received no satisfactory explanations. She became so confused and distraught that she called off the engagement.

Unfortunately she was not left with her decision founded on good judgment. Some well-intentioned friends tried to make her change her mind, claiming that breaking the engagement was grossly unfair to the "good Doctor" and would malign his reputation—so she had a moral obligation to keep her promise and marry him. Although not completely convinced by these arguments, Emma felt conscience-bound to go through with the marriage, and she became Mrs. Christopher Yates on September 18, 1838.

Fortunately for her future financial status, Emma wisely insisted on setting up a marriage agreement beforehand. She placed the management of the seminary in the hands of her son John and his wife Sarah. A large portion of her property and income was protected by being put under the care of trustees. Without this provision, her husband could have gained control of all her assets, for then there were no laws governing the retention of property rights for married women. Dr. Yates was given no choice in the arrangement; however, he married Emma in spite of the marriage agreement, apparently holding a hope of wresting the money away from his wife after the wedding. A scant two hours after the ceremony, he showed his true colors by brazenly ordering his wife to pay for the wedding feast.

When Emma refused his demands to turn over to him the proceeds of her school, her husband became an enraged tyrant. The couple's friends were unaware of the true situation because the doctor maintained the mien of a courteous gentleman away from the hearthside. He was determined to live in comfort at his wife's expense. Emma's life became a nightmare as her world seemed to be crumbling around her. It was her pride and a sense of decency which kept her from telling their friends that her husband was at fault.

Sarah was totally in the dark about the state of affairs, in fact she thought the marriage was ideal. When Dr. and Mrs. Yates moved to Boston, no one was more pleased than she. To have Emma living close by was an unexpected pleasure. The move turned out to be the ruination of what should have been a lasting friendship between the two women because for some unknown reason the doctor decided to cause a rift in their close relationship. He told Sarah in his most charming and confidential manner that his wife was making him very unhappy by insisting on teaching against his will. Sarah must have realized that in a dispute between husband and wife, a third person's opinion rarely helps the situation and often is spurned and resented, and yet she was convinced that she acted only out of her love for Emma in telling her she was at fault. The unfair criticism from her best friend was a crushing blow, an almost fatal one to their friendship. Irreparable damage might have been avoided, leaving the door open a crack for a future reconciliation but for one unforeseen circumstance—a chance meeting between the editor and the doctor, a meeting which was blown out of all proportion. Emma became convinced that Sarah had betrayed their friendship and could never forgive her.

By 1840, the year the meeting took place, Emma was legally separated from her husband but not divorced. Sarah knew nothing about the separation when she attended the Harvard commencement in the spring. Although William would not be graduated till the following year, many Bostonians went to the popular event—some without even knowing a student in attendance. There is no evidence that Sarah went to the exercises with Dr. Yates, but they did sit together, and when Emma was told this, she turned against Sarah for good.

Soon after the Harvard incident Sarah learned just how mistaken she had been in her assessment of the character of Emma's husband, and though she tried in every possible way to repair the harm her misunderstanding had caused, Emma felt Sarah had let her down at a time she desparately needed a good friend, and she refused to consider a reconciliation. The two women met only once after their estrangement.

Emma's chance meeting with Sarah took place in March of 1846. By that time Sarah was living in Philadelphia and Emma was visiting briefly in the city. One evening at dusk as Mrs. Willard was returning to her hotel, she saw Mrs. Hale sitting at the window of her boarding house, and on an impulse went in to see her. She wrote Mrs. Sigourney about this meeting.

> "I reflected how lately I had been on the brink of eternity, and our Savior's precepts of love to all—no matter how they had treated us came to my mind—and she was sitting as if she might be pensive and sorrowful. I alighted—inquired for her—and she came forward—'Who is this?' said she for it was almost dusk—Emma Willard said I—she sprang forward and embraced me with real feeling. She knew I doubt not that she had not deserved this attention at my hands. She and Josepha came in the evening with her youngest son to the hotel … and I never saw Mrs. Hale when she appeared better. But though I do not wish to

quarrel and feel the Scriptures injunctions to live in peace
— yet there is little pleasure in intercourse where confidence is lost ... But yet I have long been acquainted with
Mrs. Hale and have loved her, and I wish her well, and
rather be at peace with every human being and even with
brute creation than to live in quarrels."

Although the two women never met again, Sarah continued
to support the Troy Seminary and Emma's theories on education
in the Lady's Book. In 1874, four years after Emma's death, Sarah
paid a final tribute to her former friend when she reviewed the first
biography of the famous educator. "We commend this book to
our readers. We are glad to call attention to the memorial of a life
so useful, so honored, and so beloved as that of Emma Willard."
How very much and how sincerely Sarah had sorrowed over the
lost friendship.

Towards the end of 1838 Sarah was seriously considering a
move to Philadelphia even though William was still in Harvard.
Business responsibilities had so often put distance between the
other family members that she was reluctant to let this happen
with William, but there seemed no choice. Communications between her Boston office and the Philadelphia publishing firm were
often difficult, resulting in numerous inaccuracies, and the delays
caused by slow and undependable mail service were costly as well
as frustrating.

Christmas of 1838 was a joyous occasion for Sarah, for she
had all of her family except Horatio with her. Horatio had left
with Captain Charles Wilkes on the first United States Exploring
Expedition to the Antarctic, an assignment that would keep him
away for four years. Sarah was so proud of his appointment as
philologist to the exploration that, although she missed him very
much, his absence did not dim the festivities. And she had David
back at home after his four years in Florida. The ordeal of fighting
in the Seminole War was behind her son, and his two sisters and
William were as thrilled to have him at home as she was.
Christmas in New England was a special treat for David too — a
white Christmas with his family.

Just after the first of the year, David was ordered to the Canadian border because of the dispute with Great Britain over the steamer Caroline. Sarah was alarmed with these orders coming so soon after David's long stay in the South. He had come down with a heavy cold and she thought the sudden climate change might worsen his condition. David felt duty-bound to go. Sarah's worst fears were realized when her son became gravely ill. He died on April thirtieth in Plattsburg, New York; David was only twenty-five years old.

The same question that had brought so much anguish with the loss of her husband plagued Sarah again. "Why David in the prime of his life?" Mother and son had enjoyed a unique relationship, a closeness born in the early days of Sarah's widowhood. Young David was not quite eight when his father died, but he had tried to fulfill the role of "man of the family" in a mature and conscientious way. He was the only one of the children old enough to understand in part the depth of his mother's grief, and Sarah had found him a great comfort. Once more she prayed for sustaining strength and courage during her bereavement.

She could not possibly consider a move to Philadelphia at this time of sorrow. In a letter to Louis Godey she wrote "It is not a common loss that I mourn.... I depended on him as a friend.... I cannot, at once, summon the fortitude to enter upon the occupations of a world so dark and desolate as this now appears." With Horatio thousands of miles away and with Frances and Josepha at boarding school, Sarah wanted more than ever to have William close by.

During the hot summer months Sarah was so preoccupied with the difficult adjustment of facing a life without David that she was unable to concentrate on her work for the magazine. Schools for girls, child welfare projects, the improvement of woman's sphere of influence—all of her pet causes were eclipsed by the depth of her grief. A comparison of her present security with the pitiful circumstances at the time of her first great loss did not ease her heartache in the least; her head could tell her how very much she had to be thankful for, but the knowledge of her improved financial status would not bring David back. He had always been the one she turned to for advice in family matters when she wanted an opinion from a man's point of view. Now he was gone.

As the cooling fall breezes brought relief to the city, she regained some of her composure and with it a determination to resume her full editorial duties hoping that the normal pressures of her job and the time-consuming work would remedy her depression.

In 1841 William was graduated from Harvard, second in his class. He decided to stay on at the college for another year of studies. This decision did not alter his mother's plans to move to Philadelphia after his graduation. Frances had finished her studies, and she moved to Philadelphia with her mother. "My regret at leaving Boston was great, for my residence there had been a happy one," Sarah wrote years later in Godey's *Lady's Book*, "but it was necessary for me to be nearer the publication office of the 'Lady's Book,' and my health had suffered in the cold New England climate."

In the wintertime Sarah had minded the bone-chilling bite of the cold east wind off the ocean much more than the heavy snows of New Hampshire. Yet when a list is made of all her many and varied accomplishments during her thirteen Boston years, the causes and projects she sponsored and promoted in addition to her busy schedule as an editor and a writer, it seems difficult to envision her ever suffering from poor health. Add to all her achievements her active social life and it becomes easy to understand why one writer said, "There must have been several 'Mrs. Hales'!" Although her role in the completion of the Bunker Hill Monument was not the most significant of her prodigious achievements during this period, Sarah always felt that the "Big Fair" was the crowning glory of her Boston years.

12   Philadelphia

"By the way, there is something very pleasant and impressive in the regularity of the streets and the uniformity of the dwellings in this nice city." Sarah told her readers shortly after her move to Philadelphia. "It seems the abode of order, the place of brotherhood." Just before the move she had made a trip from Boston to Cincinnati by rail, packet, and steamboat and she was giving an enthusiastic account of some of the impressions of her journey in her "Editor's Table." She had found in all the cities visited one common denominator: the predominance of law and order. The moral integrity of people everywhere left Sarah feeling very optimistic about the state of the country.

To illustrate the distinctive manner in which individual communities seek physical improvements, she contrasted her newly adopted home "town" with New York City. "To be sure there is an apparent difference between New York, where all is 'bustle, brick, and business,' where every man seems ambitious of making or spending a fortune, and Philadelphia, looking as calm and dignified as a retired gentleman who feels himself rich enough for comfort and does not care for show."

Philadelphia in 1841 may have looked calm and dignified, but the Quaker city was in the heyday of her reign as the publishing capital of the nation, overshadowing both Boston and New York. The flourishing magazine and newspaper businesses had lured top-notch writers, artist, engravers, and editors to the city of opportunity. George Childs could boast that his *Public Ledger* was the leading daily newspaper in America and the *Port Folio*, that unique weekly which so effectively combined literature with politics, was known far and wide. One artist who had sparked magazine popularity was the engraver John Sartain whose colorful illustrations graced many periodicals. The roster of publishers and editors who contributed to the golden decade of the forties included Morton McMichael, the Peterson brothers, Abraham Hart, the Carey brothers and their brother-in-law Isaac Lea, Joseph C. Neal, Edgar Allan Poe, Sarah Hale, Louis Godey, and a newcomer—George Graham.

During the first half of the nineteenth century, many magazines were started in Philadelphia; some fought a losing battle for survival while others changed hands, character, and sometimes name to become more stable publications. Two of the latter were Atkinson's *Casket* and Burton's *Gentleman's Magazine*, both works of little merit until George Graham bought them late in 1839, combined the two and made *Graham's Magazine* the liveliest and most popular periodical of its kind in the country—and the rival of Godey's *Lady's Book*.

Godey and Graham were the first magazine owners to recognize the full monetary value of an important author and both were willing to pay top fees to secure the most celebrated literati of the day. Much to Godey's frustration, his rival was more successful in securing the work of prominent writers because there were many who hesitated to place the products of their "genius" in a woman's magazine and yet jumped with alacrity to be included in *Graham's*.

In the *House of Seven Gables*, Hawthorne gave both Godey's and Graham's periodicals a measure of permanent recognition by placing the two magazines side by side on the table in a room he was describing. In 1845 they shared something far more significant when both owners took out copyrights to protect magazine content. This action caused quite a stir in publishing circles, especially among the men who put out annuals and were in the habit of collecting the works of many writers and publishing them verbatim without paying for the privilege. Newspaper and annual publishers lashed out against this innovation. An editorial in the *Baltimore Visitor* said,

> It pains us to see that Mr. Godey has resorted to the nar-
> rowly selfish course of taking out a *copyright* for his book.
> He will rue it bitterly. Think of this insulting proposition.
> 'We have no objection to any paper copying from our
> magazine *if they will not do it until the succeeding number
> has been published.'* Wonderful liberality, Mr. Godey,
> towards that department of the press to which you are
> more or less indebted for a handsome fortune.

Naturally Sarah defended her employer's point of view, for
she had been against piracy from the beginning of her editorial
career. Another person who defended Godey was Poe, who was
editor of the *Broadway Journal* at the time.

> To our comprehension, a mere statement of the facts of the
> case should stand in lieu of all arguments. It has long been
> the custom among newspapers—especially the week-
> lies—to copy articles in full, and circulate them all over the
> country—sometimes in advance of the magazines them-
> selves. In other words Godey and Graham have been to all
> the cost, while the papers have enjoyed all the
> advantages.... To such extent has this piracy been carried
> out that many magazine subscribers have ceased to be
> such, because they could procure all that was valuable in
> these works from the newspapers....

Success had come too quickly to young Graham, wealth too
suddenly. He began speculating by buying part or whole interest
in numerous periodicals, and then he spent his earnings on ex-
travagant living. Nothing was too good for him; he bought a state-
ly mansion on Mulberry Street, and this became the scene of lavish
parties. Literary luminaries visiting the city were entertained in
grand style by the very personable young businessman. As he
drove about the Quaker city in his elegant carriage drawn by a
handsome pair of horses, Philadelphians pointed with pride to
their fine publisher, "the richest in America." Then the bubble
burst. One business venture after another lost money or failed
completely. Graham learned too late that he had spread his energy
and his money too thin. In 1848 he was forced to sell his mansion,

his "carriage and pair," and even his magazine. That year marked the end of prosperity for George Graham, and his magazine was never again the rival of the *Lady's Book*. Godey could boast, "Hundreds of magazines have been started and after a short life have departed while the 'Lady's Book' alone stands triumphant, a proud monument reared to the Ladies of America as a testimony to their worth."

Louis Godey had not fallen into the same expansion trap. His brief entry into the newspaper business came to an end in 1839 before he had jeopardized the financial security of his *Book*. He sold the weekly *Saturday News* to Samuel Atkinson who merged it with his *Saturday Evening Post*. By the time Sarah arrived in Philadelphia, Mr. Godey was devoting all of his talents to his pride and joy, his *Lady's Book*.

The publishing offices of the *Lady's Book* were on the corner of Seventh and Chestnut Streets, less than two city blocks from Sarah's lodgings at the Markos House, 919 Chestnut Street. Her reputation as a leading editor and writer opened many doors for Sarah, and her friendship with the Godeys also helped widen her range of acquaintances quickly making her feel at home. The Godeys were Episcopalians and soon after the move, Sarah joined their church.

Although Josepha was still training to be a teacher, Frances had finished her schooling, and she lived with her mother until, three years later, a handsome young naval surgeon, Dr. Louis Boudinot, made Frances his wife. The couple chose Philadelphia as their home, pleasing Sarah very much. By this time Josepha was teaching in Georgia, gaining valuable experience to prepare for opening a school of her own in Philadelphia.

William was also teaching, but in 1846 he decided to study law. After practicing his profession for a while in Virginia, William moved to Texas and settled in Galveston. His expert handling of old Spanish claims arising when Texas separated from Mexico gained him favorable recognition and led to a judgeship on the Texas Supreme Court.

Horatio had completed his work for the Wilkes' expedition by the time of his sister's marriage and was writing his first book on *Ethnography and Philology*. On the return trip from Antarctica via the Pacific, Horatio had landed at many points to study local dialects. At the mouth of the Columbia River, he left the expedition to make a solo journey inland to learn about the language differences in the remote Oregon Territory. His scientific records were helpful to the government during the dispute with Great Britain over this area.

13   1841-1850

In July of 1841 Sarah answered the request of a mother of six girls for specific directions about child rearing with an editorial, "How to Begin." It dealt mainly with physical well-being, the editor explaining that it is difficult to lay down specific rules governing education in the home because individual needs vary so greatly. "The mother must study, not books or rules, as much as the temperament and disposition of her children, and the effects which her treatment and the circumstances that surround her and them produce, day by day, on their feelings and character." Did the mother of six girls and other readers understand this advanced thinking? One wonders how this advice was received.

Sarah could be specific in her recommendations regarding good health and she backed up her opinions with quotations from a new book by a Glascow physician, *Rules for Invigorating the Constitution*. The doctor said that girls should be given as much freedom of action as boys enjoyed—not forced to walk sedately but be "allowed to run, leap, throw the ball, and play battledore, as they please." He also recommended dancing as the best indoor exercise and Sarah concurred even though dancing was a touchy subject as many Victorians felt it could arouse "animal passions."

Another recommendation in the physician's book was for daily bathing with soap and water—*all over*, a novel idea. Sarah had spoken in favor of weekly bathing and she thought the doctor's suggestion was an excellent one. After a proper diet for the growing girl was discussed, the doctor said that every girls' boarding school should have a large playground where the students could exercise and play for several hours each day.

Playgrounds, spaces for exercising in the sunshine, were very much on Sarah's mind that first oppressively hot summer in Philadelphia. Walking to and from her office she was grateful for the shade trees growing along the busy street, but she missed the broad open stretch of the Boston Common and the happy sight of children at play on the rich green carpet of grass. Where could the children of this city find such freedom to enjoy the simple pleasures of nature? There was no Frog Pond in which to wade and sail their small boats. In the public square "Keep Off the Grass" signs forced the little ones to walk only on the sun-hot gravel paths. The more she thought about this unhappy situation, the more Sarah felt some action should be taken. Her first positive step was taken the following July. That month in her "Conversation" on the editorial page she expressed her thought through three fictional characters—the schoolmaster, Ellen Marvin, and her mother.

The schoolmaster, who boarded with the Marvins, cited the lack of playground space in Philadelphia as one reason why the mortality for their city's children was higher than for Boston youngsters. Then he added

> There was much truth to the fable of Antaeus; we gain strength by touching the earth. Rural sports are indispensable for the young. How I pity little creatures who are confined in close dwellings during the pleasant weather. No matter if their parents are rich, I call such children poor; for they will never have the best feelings of heart and mind cultivated and strengthened, those which lead us to love and study nature....

In this indirect way Sarah first made her appeal for city playgrounds and she continued making these requests over the next seven years—unsuccessfully. In a May 1849 editorial she took a firmer stand with a more positive approach, widening her vision to include all cities rather than just Philadelphia. "There are squares... not yet laid out in walks.... What beautiful playgrounds for children these fresh, pleasant places would be!"

Concurrent with her attempt to improve the environmental conditions of children imprisoned in the sweltering cities, Sarah was trying to overcome some of the unhealthy attitudes of her Victorian compatriots who thought that physical frailty was attractive. Utter nonsense, said Sarah. Posh! She had been preaching this over the years in stories, essays, and in a department called "Health and Beauty." Her efforts met with some success. "We are now glad to report the progress of our own ideas; we rejoice that the good work of instructing women how to take care of themselves, of each other, and their children, is now rapidly going on."

One popular fashion that Sarah thought was very detrimental to health was the tight bodice. Time and time again the fashions in Godey's featured wasp-waisted ladies, much against the editor's better judgment. How could these young ladies breathe deeply, let alone move with any freedom? In Philadelphia, as before in Boston, she courageously spoke her piece about the fashions which did not combine health and beauty. "Ages of misery would be too little punishment," she declared, "for him who made the fashion world believe that a small waist is essential to beauty."

During the fifties two causes Sarah sponsored were treated in entirely different ways. Her support of Elizabeth Blackwell, the first woman surgeon in America, was assertive, even militant; but her pitch for women trained as mid-wives was contrastingly low keyed. Sarah knew first hand how capable a mid-wife could be, for her Great-aunt Love (Freelove Buell Nettleton) had served the town of Newport in this capacity for over ten years, before the arrival in 1790 of the first resident male physician, Dr. James Corbin. Mrs. Nettleton had most of the qualifications of a full-fledged doctor, and she administered to the whole community not only to women. Aunt Love was a warm-hearted, sympathetic woman who became a legendary figure in her own day, and tales of her courage and dedication lived on long after her death. Sarah had often heard stories about the distances her aunt traveled, sometimes on foot or horseback and in the winter on snowshoes or by sleigh, to deliver a baby, tend the sick, or give comfort in times of bereavement. Many communities depended on valiant women like Love Nettleton, but that was before the art of mid-wifery went down hill. Men had been forced to take over this role owing to the lack of women instructed in obstetrical care.

In an article written to help change this situation, Sarah took the opportunity to praise *Dr.* Elizabeth Blackwell who had graduated from Geneva College in New York in May of 1848. "She received a full degree, Doctor of Medicine, the first ever bestowed on a woman in America. She had well won it, the President of Geneva College complimented her publicly on her extraordinary attainments, and her thesis on Ship Fever was so ably written that the Faculty of Geneva determined to publish it."

This wonderful progress did not end the new doctor's struggle. Her attempt to enter the medical profession as a surgeon met with violent criticism by both the press and the clergy. Breaking ground to change the status quo almost always meets with stubborn resistance—women doctors! Sarah's defense caused as much furor in the press as her former stand on Bunker Hill. In answer to a newspaper article that claimed the editor of the *Lady's Book* was trying to starve men out of the medical profession, she wrote in the January 1853 edition of the *Book*: "It is said 'women cannot...at all times...go abroad to attend the sick.... What shall they do when they are called for and cannot go?' Just what male doctors do when they are called for and cannot go," she replied. "Stay at home!"

Sarah was aroused, infuriated. "Another says, 'You will...drive men out of the medical profession, and even those in it will starve.' "

The editor's response was, "they may as well starve as the women. And if men cannot cope with women in the medical profession let them take an humble occupation in which they can."

Another health-related project during Sarah's first decade in Philadelphia was the training of women medical missionaries. She originated the idea and steadfastly pleaded this cause in the face of violent objections. In November of 1851 she organized the Ladies' Medical Missionary Society of Philadelphia with high hopes of seeing young women with medical degrees serving as missionaries in foreign lands. At a much later date, Sarah made the comment that her action was taken "years before public opinion was ripe for it." At first, success seemed only a few short years away because some young women immediately enrolled at the Female Medical College of Philadelphia with the earnest intention of going into the missionary field, but there were still serious set-backs to be faced. Two graduates of the college, the Misses Thayer and Shattuck, were informed that they could not go abroad as missionaries unless they married first. Missionary Boards refused to sanction sending unmarried women overseas. The ladies adamantly refused to enter into wedlock just to satisfy this requirement, and so the worthwhile project was stalemated. Finally in 1869 the Foreign Missionary Board of the Methodist Church agreed to allow "Miss Swain, the first lady with a full medical diploma to go out in a missionary capacity to the Women of the East." It had taken eighteen years to drive a wedge into the secular resistance to Sarah's medical missionary proposal, but this wedge caused a successful breakthrough. Many well-qualified women followed in the footsteps of the courageous Miss Swain.

1830-1850. The *Book* was twenty years old. To celebrate the occasion, anniversary editions were published in February and December. The February number featured a portrait of the publisher with a brief biographical sketch and a capsule history of the popular periodical.

> Twenty years ago—can it be so long?—a magazine of elegant literature was cast, doubtingly, upon the uncertain stream of public favor—its name the *'Lady's Book,'* and Louis A. Godey the publisher. It was a novel enterprise at the time, and few thought it would outlive the first year of its nativity. It soon became apparent, however, that its management was in the hands of one who knew the want of the time, and had the tact and taste required for its supply.

Each year saw improvements both in content and sales. What amazed the reading public was Godey's ability to add more and more features and elaborate engravings without increasing the price. "The secret lay in the immense circulation of the 'Book,' tens of thousands of copies of which were distributed in all parts of the country. From each there was a very small profit; but the aggregate made a handsome return to the liberal-minded publisher." The article stressed, in addition to Godey's generosity and business acumen, his integrity and sincerity; he was "a fast friend and a good citizen."

In the December issue appeared a painting of Sarah along with a few words of praise by Louis Godey. His write-up gave only a few details about her life story, for "Mrs. Hale insists that her history must not appear in the *Lady's Book* while she remains its editor." He spoke mainly about her writing accomplishments, all in a most flattering manner. Then he closed the account with a recent quote from a Massachusetts newspaper.

> Mrs. Sarah J. Hale, the lady editor, is one of the most sensible and energetic of all the conductors of the numerous magazines that are now published; and as she was the pioneer in this species of literature, no one has had a greater influence, or become more universally popular among her countrywomen. Her success is richly deserved, and her energy, devotion, and perseverance under circumstances the most trying, afford a cheerful example to her sex.

Sarah was sixty-two years old when her portrait by Chambers was engraved in her magazine. A picture speaks a somewhat different message to each beholder; however, writers commenting on the painting have remarked on Sarah's extremely youthful appearance. Lawrence Martin saw "a woman of not more than forty" and Ruth Finley said the editor seemed "almost too youthful, too animated, for a woman past sixty," and yet daguerreotypes taken at later periods in her life bore out the accuracy of the artist's depiction. Sarah looks out from the painting with the forthright gaze of a woman who knows who she is and where she is going, and the smile playing around the corners of her mouth gives evidence of her lively sense of humor, her zest for life.

That December of 1850 Sarah had been an editor for twenty-two years, but this would be less than half of her long career. Her success had been great and richly deserved and yet some of her most noteworthy achievements still lay in the future.

14   Mount Vernon

"A noble plan has been formed for securing to the people of America the 'Home and Grave of the Father of our Country.' " Sarah made this pronouncement in the August *Lady's Book* in 1855. In her elaboration of the subject, she proudly stated that it was a woman who had initiated the project and that the glorious enterprise would meet with success if women across the nation rallied to support the cause.

The Mount Vernon Association was started by a woman, true, but it was man who first called Sarah's attention to the sad condition of the Mount Vernon buildings "dilapidated and decaying... overgrown with briars... a scene of wreck and waste." In 1849 two rooms of the Mount Vernon mansion, the Great Entrance Hall and the Great Hall, were pictured in Godey's and these engravings may have led the reporter Robert Criswell, Jr., to make a trip to Mount Vernon and write an article for the *Lady's Book*. When he sent in his editorial for publication, Sarah was appalled to learn of the neglect which had caused so much deterioration, and even more appalled to read in that account that the owner, John Augustine Washington, was planning to sell off the land and buildings in a month if no one stepped in to save the property for a national shrine. Criswell explained the situation.

"Congress had been petitioned again and again to purchase Mount Vernon, but as yet to no effect. The present owners are willing to dispose of one hundred and fifty acres, including the buildings, tombs, and immediate grounds for about one hundred thousand dollars." This was a very generous offer in light of the fact that John Washington had already been offered three hundred thousand by speculators. He turned down this offer because of his strong belief that the buildings and property should be converted into a national shrine to honor the "Father of Our Country." Criswell said that "If Congress is unwilling to appropriate the necessary funds from the public treasury, let it appoint suitable agents, and the amount can be raised by private subscriptions in one month...."

One short month! Sarah lost no time writing to Virginia for more information. What steps was Congress taking? None! The property was not sold at the end of a month—neither to Congress nor to speculators—and the buildings continued to go down hill and the weeds continued to prosper. Under these circumstances one wonders why Sarah did not take Mount Vernon under her wing as she had the Bunker Hill project. George Washington was at the top of her list of patriotic heroes and the saving of his home and grave was, in her estimation, an extremely worthwhile cause. Yet she took no action in 1849.

The next episode in the Mount Vernon saga took place four years later. A woman from South Carolina was on a Potomac River steamboat returning from a Philadelphia visit with her daughter Anne Pamela. Mrs. Cunningham was in very low spirits after a sad parting with her invalid daughter. Anne had been a southern belle with all the world at her feet until she had a horseback riding accident in her teens. Her spine was severely injured when she was thrown to the ground. Now twenty-one years and many doctors' visits later, there was little improvement in her condition. Mrs. Cunningham left her daughter for the winter under the care of an excellent physician, Dr. Hodge, no longer hoping for a cure but knowing that the doctor had a calming effect that alleviated Anne's depression and gave her the courage to go on.

As her ship steamed down the Potomac at night, the tolling of the bell which signaled that they were passing Mount Vernon brought Anne's mother out onto the deck. "The moon was full in the sky; in its soft radiance the impressive features of the once lovely spot were plainly visible—the mansion, the tomb; more poignantly the air of desolation brooding over all." She envisioned the estate as Washington had known and loved it, and the contrast with the depressing scene which met her glance saddened her immeasurably. The next day she wrote about this painful experience to Anne saying that it was a disgrace the way our country was letting the site go to ruin. During the night an idea had come to her. If Congress and the State of Virginia refused to act, maybe the women of the South could band together and raise the money to save the relic.

This letter was the start of a lifelong crusade for the semi-invalid who decided to put her mother's idea into action by writing a letter to the Charleston *Mercury* appealing to the women of the South to save Mount Vernon. The long and impassioned newspaper appeal was signed "A Southern Matron." Anne had told her friend Virginia Hall about her choice of signature. When Virginia laughingly exclaimed "You are not a Southern matron!," Anne replied that her mother was and "as I dislike publicity, no one will recognize me under that name... ."

The *Mercury* letter asked each woman in the South to contribute "a mite" so that the land and buildings could be purchased and "conveyed to the President of the United States and to the Governor of Virginia" to become a hallowed shrine for all Americans. Anne suggested further that once this had been accomplished, continued preservation and improvement could be maintained by charging visitors a "trifle," a noble plan but one which was to be fraught with many obstacles along the way.

Anne's appeal in the *Mercury* aroused spontaneous interest, and the Mount Vernon Association was formed with the "Southern Matron" as president. For two years the women worked diligently to raise funds; however, the amount realized was a mere drop compared to the huge sum required. The price John Washington was willing to sell the estate for had doubled to two hundred thousand dollars. The association's members decided they would have to gain national recognition and support. In 1855 they asked two periodicals to represent them in the fund raising drive, the *Southern*

Literary Messenger for their area and in the North Godey's *Lady's Book*. Sarah told her readers in August that the *Book* had accepted the appointment and that she hoped to interest all her friends "in this great effort of national patriotism."

Like most thoughtful Americans in the mid-century, Sarah was gravely concerned about the ever-increasing tension between the North and the South, tension she had foreseen in 1827 when she wrote *Northwood*. All her life she had felt very strongly about the sanctity of the Union, believing its preservation ranked above all other considerations. Could the women of both sections of the country uniting in a common cause help ease the growing alienation? Sarah put her whole heart into the effort to save Mount Vernon.

> We want contributions from every section—we want the daughters of the North to come, with rich gifts and join their sisters of the South, as the brave patriots of both regions united in the glorious war of the Revolution. Washington's fame belongs to his whole country—his name is the holy cement of our Union. ... Every donation sent to us shall be registered, and with the *name* of the giver, if not prohibited, enrolled in our 'Book.' We shall furnish monthly accounts of the progress of this grand enterprise in every part of our Union, and we do earnestly hope that each and all of the 'Old Thirteen' will unite in that beautiful spirit of emulation which seeks to excel in well-doing.

Month after month Sarah reported the progress of the association, and requested one-dollar membership subscriptions from every reader. Not just the women were approached by the enthusiastic editor. "How we wish that liberal men, who love the memory of Washington, would send donations of $1000 each, to encourage the work! We will set such names in the largest capitals our 'Book' allows."

In January 1856 Sarah was pleased to relate how "deeply gratified" the association members were by all the interest that had been created in furthering their cause, adding that the women were cheered by the encouraging prospects of final success. Money had been received by individuals "in every portion of our country, from New England to Louisiana," and there was even more exciting news. Swelling with pride, Sarah told her readers about the wonderful example her adopted city had set for other localities by joining the Ladies' Association. It seemed very fitting that Philadelphia's patriots "with the spirit of '76 still animating their hearts" should be the first to answer "woman's earnest appeal," for no city in the Union had had any closer ties with the military and civil career of George Washington.

That same month a bill was passed by the Virginia State Legislature to "Incorporate the Mount Vernon Ladies' Association of the Union, and to authorize the purchase of a part of the Mount Vernon place." Sarah was so jubilant that she had the entire bill published in the *Book*. Then just one month later an ominous note sounded in her report of progress.

> Although there has been some misunderstanding in respect to the arrangements for the purchase of the estate of Washington, yet no permanent obstacle is anticipated. The ladies are going on with their collections, confident that we shall obtain the property when we have secured the funds. How can we hesitate when we have such a coadjutor as the Hon. Edward Everett, who has gained, by his noble oration on Washington, nearly *ten thousand dollars*, which he invests for the purchase of Mount Vernon? He is intending to repeat this oration throughout the country, as all the people are pressing him to do; and the whole amount he gains is to be saved to this object.

Everett did not even take his expenses out but paid the cost of his travel from his own pocket!

The misunderstanding was more serious than Sarah had indicated, a genuine roadblock to further progress. John Washington had laid down specific directions about how he wanted the sale of his property handled. Because the Virginia Charter had not followed his instructions, he withdrew his offer to sell the estate. Public confidence in the project hit a real low with this bitter disappointment; however, the women refused to abandon hope, especially the dauntless Anne Cunningham.

As soon as she learned of the unhappy turn of events, Anne

traveled to Mount Vernon to speak with the owner in person. The journey was a difficult one owing to her poor condition. "I was carried up to Mount Vernon in a chair, on a very hot day in June, 1856.... I saw the family, was kindly received; but all my arguments failed, though Mr. Washington promised to meet me in Washington."

It was a very unhappy Anne who was carried down to the wharf, unhappier still when she discovered the boat had left without her. She was obliged to spend the night with the Washingtons. This unexpected stay proved very fortuitous for the Mount Vernon cause. During the evening Anne told the family "various incidents connected with Mr. Everett and his Washington lecture, and enlightened the family in a roundabout way as to our proceedings and the interest felt. I could see their amazement. It was a side of the shield they had not seen. I felt I had gained *Mrs.* Washington.... I counselled Mr. Washington to follow the example of his illustrious ancestor, who 'never acted on a grave affair without having slept on it.' The next morning I had a regular talk.... I never spoke to a mortal as I spoke to him." Yet her appeal did not shake his resolution against selling the property to the State of Virginia.

It was not until Anne was on the point of leaving that she struck a responsive chord.

> I told him I knew the public had behaved abominably towards him; that the Virginia Legislature had done so, also, in framing a charter contrary to the terms he had expressed himself willing to accept.... As much as the ladies wanted to succeed in their beautiful tribute, we were grieved that his feelings were hurt—insulted so repeatedly—because of it. I looked up as I said this. What a change in his face! Unaware, I had at last touched the sore spot — the obstacle that no money could have removed. I now found that he believed the whole thing had been arranged between the Association and Virginia to put an indignity on him! His feelings were wounded, goaded; and lo! in explaining my feelings, I had shown him *his* error.

John Washington still did not give Anne a positive answer,

but she promised him she would try to overcome any objections he had before approaching him with the proposition again. She left him with a warm handshake and the belief that the success of the mission was assured.

Mr. Washington's quasi-agreement was enough to fire the association members with renewed zeal, but not sufficient assurance for the general public. Sarah did her part to attempt to keep interest alive and yet contributions dwindled and finally came to a stop. In September of 1856 she promised that "In our next we shall give a paper on this subject, and give the names of contributors—." In November a short list appeared, but no paper. Although Sarah kept plugging the cause and begging for dollar donations, the response was practically nil. Everett also worked hard to build public confidence by telling his audiences that "Should the attempt to purchase Mount Vernon eventually fail, the funds raised can be appropriated to some other patriotic purpose of general interest connected with the memory of Washington." But the dream was Mount Vernon!

By the March of 1857 Sarah was able to sound a little more hopeful because she had been told that progress was being made and a report would soon be laid before the public. Then in April she wrote under the Mount Vernon heading, "This society is not idle though the Report is not yet ready." A month later all appeared smooth sailing again and Sarah stated with confidence, "There is no longer any reason to doubt the success of the plan for purchasing and preserving the home and grave of Washington." Great news, but a bit premature as more problems were in the offing.

The money panic occurring in the fall of the year was a bitter blow. Contributions came to a halt. Fortunately a knight came to the rescue, none other than Edward Everett who had already raised thousands of dollars to save Mount Vernon. The lecturer spoke in cities and towns in every state across the nation. His final contribution totaled almost seventy thousand dollars, the largest single donation by a large margin, over one-third of the purchase price.

A new agreement was drawn up and presented to the Virginia Legislature. No one had any reason to doubt that the lawmakers would do other than sign on the dotted line. In retrospect it seems incredulous, with all the interest shown in every section of

America, that there were still enough legislators opposed to the goal of the association to defeat the bill. With the bill defeated, the project appeared doomed. It was at this point in the Mount Vernon story that the sympathetic understanding Anne Cunningham had shown to John Washington with his wounded pride really paid dividends. Anne asked the owner if he would sell the estate directly to the Ladies' Association and he acquiesced. The women made a down payment of eighteen thousand dollars with the agreement the remainder would be paid on February 22, 1859. A complete account of the transaction was published in the *Lady's Book* for August 1858.

The closing date had to be postponed a year; however, no serious snag held up the project and Sarah was thrilled to write in March of 1860, "MOUNT VERNON now belongs to the American nation." The women had made the final payment and their goal was secured. The effort had united the whole country at a most critical point in our nation's history. Although it was impossible to ignore the distant beat of approaching war drums, Sarah expressed a sincere hope that the success of the patriotic triumph was "the happy harbinger of faith in the permanence of our National Union."

15 Thanksgiving Day

The establishment of an annual national Thanksgiving Day seemed like such an excellent idea to Sarah that there was no way she could have envisioned it would take thirty-six long years from conception to fruition, years during which she would write thousands of personal letters, hundreds of editorials, and experience countless disappointments as each November rolled around without the accomplishment of her cherished goal.

The idea of a national Thanksgiving celebration did not originate with Sarah. In 1789 Washington had issued the first proclamation setting aside the last Thursday in November for a "Day of Thanksgiving and prayer" and she frequently quoted from this document over the years; but his was a one-time event and Sarah wished to make the day an annual festival. Seventy-four years went by after George Washington's proclamation before Abraham Lincoln wrote the second Thanksgiving proclamation—*at Sarah's request*. (This little known fact does not appear in our history books.)

It was in the year of 1827 that she first stated her wish in *Northwood*, and the wording sounded very optimistic. The hero's father, Squire Romilly, answered his English guest's query "Is Thanksgiving Day universally observed in America?" by saying "Not yet, but I trust it will soon become so. We have too few holidays. Thanksgiving Day, like the Fourth of July, should be considered a national festival and observed by all our people." Then embellishing his point in true Victorian fashion, the squire added that when Thanksgiving "shall be observed, on the same day, throughout all the states and territories, it will be a grand spectacle of moral power and human happiness, such as the world has never witnessed."

The Thanksgiving dinner the Romillys served their guest was based on ones Sarah had so much enjoyed on the Buells' East Mountain farm, and what a hearty feast it was. "The roast turkey took precedence on this occasion, being placed at the head of the table and well did it become its lordly station, sending forth the rich odor of its savory stuffing and finely covered with the froth of basting." A palate-tempting list of staples and delicacies, all home grown and prepared, included a large chicken pie, three kinds of meat, a goose, and a pair of ducklings which were served with "innumerable bowls of gravy and plates of vegetables...." Pickles, preserves, and fine wine were part of the feast and that was only the first course. "A side table was literally loaded with the preparations for the second course.... There was a huge plum pudding, custards and pies of every name and description ever known in Yankee land; yet the pumpkin occupied the most distinguished niche. There were also several kinds of rich cakes, and a variety of sweetmeats and fruits." The dinner played an important role in the celebration of Thanksgiving, second only to the religious aspect of the holiday. Thanking the Great Provider at a morning church meeting and then once more in a lengthy grace before the meal gave the Day its significance.

It was this religious element that Sarah stressed in early magazine editorials asking for the establishment of an annual national observance of Thanksgiving. Then in 1835 a social dimension was added. "There is a deep moral influence in these periodical seasons of rejoicing, in which whole communities participate."

Sarah did not begin an all-out Thanksgiving Day campaign until 1846. During the previous summer she had been invited to take part in a Fourth of July celebration in her native town of Newport. "We had been absent many years," she told her *Lady's Book* readers. "Not a relative remained to welcome us, and but a few of our early associates — yet it was *home* still. The green hills and the bright river were there; the remembered places of childhood and youth...."

The editor told her readers that she thought the Newport

celebration was the first time a town had invited former residents to participate in an anniversary event, and she hoped other communities would follow this "mode of keeping national jubilee."

This hometown gathering gave Sarah greater determination to realize her cherished Thanksgiving Day goal. Her editorial that November was followed by one the next year which placed her plan squarely before her public. She said she would use the *Book* as the instrument to plug for a nation-wide celebration.

"As this is a subject in which ladies should take a deep interest, will it be thought presumptuous if our 'Book,' as their special organ, leads the way in the good work of union in Thanksgiving?" Then, feeling that the answer must assuredly be a resounding "No, of course it is not presumptuous!" she suggested that "from this year, 1847, henceforth and forever, as long as the Union endures, the *last Thursday of November be the Day* set apart by every State for its annual Thanksgiving. Will not the whole press of the country advocate this suggestion?"

From that year on, at least two editorials were printed on her pet project; one was published early in the year calling for cooperation from all state and territorial governors, and then another appeared in November evaluating the measure of her success and asking for more states to join in this project before another November.

Sarah also wrote letters to governors, congressmen, and other influential people across the country asking for support. The first president to receive one of her letters was Zachary Taylor in 1852. No action was taken. By 1852 she could report some progress; twenty-nine states and all the territories had participated the previous year. "This year," she wrote, "we trust that Virginia and Vermont will come into the arrangement, and that the Governors of each and all States and Territories will appoint *Thursday, the 25th of November, as the Day of Thanksgiving.*"

Sarah's failure to interest President Taylor in her cause had been discouraging; however, she persisted with her plan to gain support in Washington. Letters to Fillmore, Pierce, and Buchanan were equally abortive. But by 1858 enough states had joined the bandwagon to strengthen her spirits and to give her hope for final success. She added a new dimension to her plea that year.

Let us consecrate the day to the benevolence of action, by sending good gifts to the poor, and doing those deeds of charity that will, for one day, make every American home a place of plenty and rejoicing. These seasons of refreshing are of inestimable advantage to the popular heart; and, if rightly managed, will greatly aid and strengthen public harmony of feeling.

Sarah was not young when her Thanksgiving effort was a part of her very busy work schedule, but she was young looking. One of her fans, who visited Philadelphia in 1859, gave an interesting account of her reaction to Sarah's youthful appearance. Lucy Sanford had enjoyed reading *Godey's Lady's Book* "from childhood on," and she was thrilled when one of her first attempts at story writing was published by Sarah.

Lucy Sanford, twenty years later wrote,

When, therefore, in 1859, I was in Phladelphia and my sister invited Mrs. Hale to dine and go to the opera, given in compliment to the Prince of Wales, I was far more pleased to meet the lady editor, than the future king.

I expected to see an intellectual old lady, who wore glasses and talked books. I did see a charming society lady of middle age, with undimmed eye, and with a clear, broad, high, smooth forehead, with never a wrinkle or a crow's foot on it.

Before I left the city I told her how surprised I was to find her so young. She smiled, saying, "I am only seventy-one!" She said the secret of her young-old age was that she was born in the country, and played out-of-doors from morning to night.

A new note was sounded in July of 1859 when Sarah's November Thanksgiving editorial stressed the unifying effect such a national observance could have on the country. War clouds were threatening the "Rainbow of Peace," and the security of the Union was on shaky grounds. "If every State should join in union thanksgiving on the 24th of this month, would it not be a renewed pledge of love and loyalty to the Constitution of the United States, which guarantees peace, prosperity, progress and perpetuity in our great Republic?" Failure again.

One year later she wrote, "This year the *last Thursday in November* falls on the 29th. If all the States and Territories hold their Thankgiving on that day, there will be a complete moral and social reunion of the *people* of America in 1860. Would not this be a good omen for the perpetual political union of the States? May God grant us not only the omen, but the fulfillment is our dearest wish!"

The breakthrough year was 1863, and Sarah must have sensed victory, for her constant plea was absent and a new suggestion made. Her requests had always been for the governors to issue the necessary proclamations. "Would it not be better that the proclamation that appoints Thursday, the 26th of November as the Day of Thanksgiving for the people of the United States should, in the first instance, emanate from the President of the Republic—to be applied by the Governors of each and every State, in acquiescence with the chief magistrate?" Then off went her letter to President Lincoln.

The reply to her letter came from Secretary of State William Seward who wrote, "I have received your interesting letter—and have commended the same to the consideration of the President." Seward must have carried some of his enthusiasm to the president because four days after his letter was sent to Sarah, Lincoln issued his Thanksgiving Day Proclamation asking the American people to gratefully acknowledge

> as with one heart and one voice—the blessings of fruitful fields and healthful skies—. I do, therefore, invite my fellow citizens in every part of the United States and also those who are at sea or who are sojourning in foreign lands to set apart and observe the last Thursday of November next as a day of Thanksgiving and praise to our Beneficient Father who dwelleth in the heavens. And I recommend to them that while offering up the subscriptions justly due to Him for such singular deliverance and blessings, they do also with humble penitence for our natural perverseness and disobedience, commend to His tender care all those who have become widows, orphans, mourners or sufferers in the lamentable civil strife in which we are unavoidably engaged, and fervently implore the interposition of the

Almighty Hand to heal the wounds of the nation to the full
enjoyment of peace, harmony, tranquility, and Union.

Sarah's persistent effort had borne fruit at a time when our
country needed a unifying influence. In church, while Lincoln's
Proclamation was being read, she must have felt deeply grateful to
the man who had finally made her wish come true. How long she
had waited for that precious moment! Sarah was thirty-nine when
she expressed the belief that Thanksgiving Day would soon be "a
national festival and observed by all our people." In 1863 she had
reached the young-old age of seventy-five.

Surely by that late date she could rest on laurels earned from a
job well done; but no, her campaign was not finished. Two years
later when Lincoln was assassinated, Sarah feared Thanksgiving
might suffer the same fate as had occurred in 1789, and so she
posed this question to the new president, "Shall 1866 be the glorious year that establishes the custom of observing Thanksgiving
forever?" Andrew Johnson continued the practice; however, no
legislation was passed to legalize the holiday on a permanent basis.

Godey's *Lady's Book*, February of 1869. "THE NATIONAL
THANKSGIVING DAY. This great American holiday was
celebrated in 1868 almost universally throughout the Republic,"
the editor stated in her editorial "Table." The president had issued
his proclamation to thirty-five million people.

> Nor was the day observed only within our native territory.
> Of course it was kept in Alaska—the first Thanksgiving
> day ever known in that boreal region. There were
> Thanksgiving dinners in London, Paris, Liverpool,
> Frankfort, Berlin, Florence, and Rome. The traditional
> roast turkey was served up under the American flag in
> Japan at the mouth of the Amoor River, in St. Petersburg,
> and in Rio de Janeiro. The Day needs only the sanction of
> Congress to become established as an American Holiday,
> not only in the Republic, but wherever Americans meet
> throughout the world.

Sarah had one more letter to write, this time to a distant
relative, President Grant. After making her final request, the

custom of an annual national Thanksgiving Day was firmly established but not *legalized*. Congress did not pass a resolution on this issue until the third term of Franklin Roosevelt.

Thousands of Americans were more than a little upset when President Roosevelt set the third Thursday in November for the Thanksgiving celebration. Businessmen who wished a longer pre-Christmas shopping season had been eloquently persuasive and Roosevelt had bowed to their request, but twenty-three states refused to go along with the change. For the three years of the early holiday, these states observed Thanksgiving on the fourth Thursday. The fervor against the innovation was sufficiently strong to force the president to capitulate. Then and only then did Congress finally act. A joint resolution making Thanksgiving Day on the fourth Thursday in November a legal holiday was passed in 1941. At long last Sarah's cherished dream was legally established; our Thanksgiving Day was secured.

16   Vassar College

Matthew Vassar was fifty-three years old and vacationing in England when he reached a momentous decision. While visiting the London Hospital, Mr. Vassar was much impressed when he learned that the famous institution had been founded by one of his own ancestors, Sir John Guy. How wonderful to be rememberd by future generations as a benefactor of mankind. Could he gain for himself such an honored place in the annals of history?

Wanting to be remembered by posterity for good deeds is not an uncommon wish, but few visionaries so moved are in the enviable position of having a ready-made fortune to devote to the realization of their ambition. The source of Vassar's wealth was his very profitable brewery business in Poughkeepsie, New York. He had the means, and so the question became one of choosing the right philanthropic endeavor. Many interested people offered suggestions, but one made by his friend Milo Jewett seemed the perfect answer and became his final choice. Mr. Jewett told him that if he used his money "to build and endow a college for young women which shall be to them what Harvard and Yale are to young men," he would become a pioneer in the field of education and secure for himself "a monument more lasting than the pyramids." This suggestion hit a responsive chord, for the philanthropist had taken an interest in girls' schools for many years, and so he decided to follow his friend's advice and establish a women's college of the highest quality.

Sarah heard the good news in the fall of 1860, and she wasted no time in writing a letter praising the project and offering Vassar her assistance. "I shall rejoice to aid in your good plan, by making the readers of the *Lady's Book* your earnest friends as they cannot but honor a gentleman who is thus earnest to promote the true cultivation of feminine talents."

Her offer was far more valuable than mere moral support in that pre-radio and pre-television era; free magazine publicity was invaluable. Vassar, well aware of the worth of her backing, showed his appreciation by preserving Sarah's first letter in the college records. In the thank-you reply, he said, "I am honored in finding my own views so much in harmony with the Sentiments found in Editorials of the Lady's Book...." And so began a lengthy and warm correspondence between these two, letters which gave the editor ample opportunity to influence many policy-making decisions of the new college.

Almost the complete editorial department in the October 1860 issue of the *Book* dealt with plans for the new school.

> While clouds and darkness overhang the land, we naturally welcome with double pleasure whatever promises permanent good for the future. The founding of institutions like Vassar Female College, in a year like the present, is a peculiarly cheering event. This institution, as many readers are aware, owes its origin wholly to the munificent liberality of a single founder, Matthew Vassar, Esq., a wealthy and public-spirited citizen of Poughkeepsie, who has devoted a large portion of his fortune—no less than *four hundred and eight thousand dollars*—to the object of 'erecting and endowing a college for the education of young women.'

Sarah's greatest contribution, other than magazine advertisement and promotion, was in securing a place for women on the faculty. Late in 1863 a proposed outline of organization was published with no provision for women on the college staff. Sarah was greatly disappointed and wrote at once to Matthew Vassar presenting a strong case in favor of women professors. In a letter dated January 25, 1864, the founder said, "The subject of Women Professors & Teachers is now fairly before our Trustees, who at their Meeting 23rd proximo will report their views, and decide if it can be safely adopted in our College at the opening. The only question that can possibly arise, is whether we *can obtain* prominent and distinguished Lady instructors to fill the several chairs."

The case did not turn out to be so simple. Milo Jewett had been chosen the first president and he adamantly rejected the proposal on the grounds that it would be impossible to secure women qualified to be professors. The issue became a live coal. President Jewett refused to budge an inch; however, Sarah was just as determined to win her point because she felt her stand was the only valid one. She realized that a woman speaking for women might not carry as much weight with the trustees as a man's point of view and so she made a wise move.

Horatio had married a Canadian girl, Margaret Pugh, and the couple had settled in Clinton, Ontario, in 1856. Sarah wrote to her son asking him to compose an editorial on this important subject for her. Both Horatio and her grandson Richard Hunter were helping Sarah out with some of writing chores because of an eye problem caused by cataracts. (This problem, which gave her difficulty for several years, disappeared miraculously without corrective measures; the editor never wore glasses!)

Horatio sent his mother an essay entitled "VASSAR COLLEGE" with the subtitle "THE NEW PLAN OF ORGANIZATION EXAMINED; ONLY 'ONE DEFECT.' AND THIS MAY BE EASILY AMENDED." The February editorial was not signed, but in a footnote Sarah stated that "This article, contributed by a gentleman whose opportunites of understanding the subject he discusses have been of no common order, will, we hope, be carefully read. The remarks respecting the 'one defect' seem to us so just that we feel sure those who have the organization of this important college in their keeping will thank this 'friend of education,' who has fully and frankly expressed his own ideas on this subject."

Horatio used his mother's technique of first praising the good points of the plan before stating its one shortcoming.

> In the whole scheme of organization we remark only one defect; but that is of such a serious nature that we hope to see it amended before the plan is finally adopted. It would

seem that not only the President but all the teachers are to be men. The only women for whom offices are proposed are some 'assistant teachers'... a Nurse, a Housekeeper and a Matron....

That the President of the new college should be a gentleman like Professor Jewett...is certainly desirable; but there should also be a Lady Superintendent who should have the more immediate control of the pupils, and all instructors should be ladies except when properly qualified teachers of that sex cannot be found....

We lay the more stress upon this consideration at present, as we trust that Vassar College will become the parent and model of many similar institutions throughout our country. Surely the President and Trustees of this college, which is designed by its generous Founder for the elevation of woman, will not commence by degrading her. They will not announce to the world that, owing to something peculiar in the character or intellect of woman (a defect now for the first time discovered), they have not been able to find a lady in the United States qualified to instruct her own sex in the higher branches of science and learning, or to take charge of a department in a College for Young Women....

Later that month Horatio's editorial was warmly debated at the board meeting of the trustees. Many men agreed with the views of Sarah and her son. The chief opponent was still President Jewett. No action was taken on the issue of a mixed faculty, and Sarah sadly reported this fact to her readers. In answer to the contention that it would be impossible to find qualified women to teach, Sarah quoted the gentleman, "a friend of woman," who had written the February article. He "has since suggested a way by which these lady candidates may be found." Horatio said the matter could easily be accomplished "if the Trustees of Vassar College would pursue a very usual course—announce in the public journals that certain professorships were to be filled by ladies, state the salary to be given, and the qualifications required, and call upon aspirants to send the proper testimonials...." He was sure, he added, that the trustees would be surprised how many applicants would come forward.

After passing this information along to her readers, Sarah penned another letter to the founder. Mr. Vassar assured her that he shared her point of view. "My desire is now and has always been to make our College, not only a College to educate Women, but a College of instruction by *women*," he wrote in March. "Will you my dear Mrs. Hale continue to support me in these views."

He was having a difficult time with his friend Milo, a problem which was not solely based on the question of a mixed faculty. There was friction between the president and another board member, the Reverend Charles Raymond, and all Vassar's earnest endeavor to make peace between the two men failed. In April President Jewett tendered his resignation, much to the sorrow of Matthew Vassar who had hoped matters would not reach such a drastic conclusion. Sarah had received the unhappy news directly from Milo Jewett, and she wrote to Mr. Vassar expressing the wish that there could have been a more amicable solution. Matthew replied that he was glad she had already heard the news as it saved him from "that painful duty" and he also told her that Dr. Raymond had been appointed as Jewett's successor.

After Dr. Raymond became president, the matter of a mixed faculty was settled much to Sarah's great satisfaction. Besides a "Lady Principal" and a resident woman physician who taught physiology and hygiene, there were many other women professors. When the college opened its doors on September 20, 1865, twenty-four women and eight men made up the teaching staff, a triumph for Sarah. She had won a major victory, even though she did lose two lesser battles.

In the first discussions about curriculum, she had recommended a course in Domestic Science. She thought the students should be given "a method of practical instruction in household knowledge and duties." But when the Record of Organization came out, she found "no trace of anything of this description." In a lengthy treatise on the subject in the January 1865 *Book*, the editor pointed out a basic difference in the college set-up for men and women.

It should be borne in mind that institutions for the education of young women differ widely, in one respect, from the ordinary colleges for young men. These colleges, for the most part, only give what may be called a preparatory course of instruction. The pupil of Harvard or Yale does not usually complete his education in his college; he passes from it to a Law, Divinity, or Medical School, or to a counting-room or engineer's office, where he spends several years in acquiring the practical knowledge required for his profession. A Seminary for young ladies is intended to complete the education of its inmates. It should therefore combine the two courses of instruction, the scientific and the practical; as every young lady expects to be, at some period of her life, a housekeeper, she should leave her College as well versed in the theory and practice of that calling as the young lawyer, physician, or divine is expected to be who leaves the 'school' or office in which he had pursued the course of studies qualifying him for his profession.

Sarah informed her readers in the organization of Vassar,

there are to be Schools of Natural History, of Physical Science, of Psychology, of Mathematics, and of Art, but none of Domestic Science. The young ladies are to undergo examinations in Mensuration, Surveying, and Navigation, and in the differential and integral calculus, which, however servicable in the way of mental discipline, will, we fear, help them very little in the actual duties of after life.

The young lawyer or merchant who has had the good fortune to carry off to his new home a fair graduate of Vassar College will doubtless be not a little proud of the intellectual acquirements of his bride. But when he comes down with a limp collar to an ill-cooked breakfast, the idea will be likely to occur to him that it would be well if the idol of his heart, in addition to so much abstract science, had acquired something more of that practical training for her actual sphere which he himself has been obliged to go through to fit him to the duties of his own calling. When matters go wrong in the kitchen or laundry, it will be no great compensation to know that the directress of these departments is fully qualified, in case of necessity, to navigate a vessel or survey a township. Even the certainty that she could, if required, calculate all the eclipses that will occur during the next century, will hardly, we fear, be deemed by the perplexed husband a sufficient consolation for her entire ignorance of the mysteries of starch and cooking.

Even with this sound argument painted with a light touch and with the backing of Matthew Vassar, no such practical course of studies was offered at the first college for women. In fact it was not until 1922 that "her course" was introduced and then it was hailed as an innovation, a great advance in the field of education for women. This was fifty-seven years after Sarah's initial proposal.

The second lost cause was a minor one and yet it seemed very important to the editor. For fifteen years she had been trying to have the use of the word "female" deleted from the English language. Although she herself had often used this connotation before 1850, about that time she became convinced the meaning was "vulgarizing our style of writing and our mode of speech." The name under consideration for the new school, Vassar Female College, had caused a great deal of controversy.

Sarah was very upset that "Female" might appear in the name of the college. Had all her work for the eradication of this offensive word been entirely in vain? Had no one paid any attention to all her editorials and comments about the derogatory connotation so demeaning to her sex? Sarah felt she was making good headway until the Vassar trustees settled on a final name choice. Over the main entrance of the new school were three huge marble stones carved with the words *VASSAR FEMALE COLLEGE.*

Sarah's reaction was vehement. "Female!" she exploded in a letter to the founder, dated March 30, 1865.

> What female do you mean? Not a female donkey? Must not your reply be 'I mean a female woman'? Then... why degrade the feminine sex to the level of animals? ...I write thus earnestly because I wish to have Vassar College take the lead in this great improvement in our language....Pray do not, my good friend, disappoint me. It is not for myself

that I expect any benefit. I plead for the good of Vassar College, for the honor of womanhood and the glory of God.

To this earnest plea, her friend replied that he approved of a name change; however, now it would require an act of legislature. Then he assured Sarah that "when the time comes for me to donate a further sum to the Institution I shall make this point (with some other matters) a condition of the Gift, which will exert an influence in the change, and thus meet out your views & mine. Whatever remarks therefore you may think proper to make in your next number of the Lady's book I hope you will do in accordance with these views but upon your *own* authority.... "

Matthew Vassar was true to his word and Sarah was most pleased to receive a letter from him as soon as progress had been made.

Poughkeepsie, June 27, 1866

My dear Mrs. Hale:

I hasten to inform you that the great agony is over—your long cherished wishes realized. Woman stands redeemed, at least so far as Vassar College is concerned, from the vulgarism in the associated name of "female."...Yesterday opened and closed the business of the college annual Trustee doings....I was called on for my customary address, one essential portion of which was to urge the change of title of the college....After some little discussion it was unanimously decided by vote to drop the middle letter [word?] to read thus — 'Vassar College'; and they appointed a committee to prepare the necessary papers for the opening of the next legislature....

Then over a year later Sarah received another letter from her friend which must have made her swell with pride. "Woman" stood "redeemed." The good-news letter was dated September 9, 1867. "...a singular coincidence just occurred on the day of receipt of your last letter the central marble slab on the front of the Edifice containing the word 'Female' was removed...." Matthew Vassar wrote, "relieving the Institution from the odium which has so long disgraced it & It now reads — *VASSAR COLLEGE* — and underneath this name "Founded A. D. 1861." The following statement must have been very heart warming to the editor of the *Lady's Book*. "...and let me assure you that to you dear friend and to you only am I indebted for this change after so long a contest by a phalanx of opposers."

17 Civil War Years

"Let us trust that the pen and not the sword will decide the controversy now going on in our land; and that any part women may take in the former mode will be promotive of peace, and not suggestive of discord." This was in the final chapter of the 1852 revision of *Northwood* that Sarah had brought out with the hope that her novel might in some measure counteract the inflammatory influence of *Uncle Tom's Cabin* which had just been published.

Harriet Beecher Stowe and Sarah were both deeply religious humanitarians who abhorred the evils of slavery and both were idealists. Sarah's proposal of a means for peaceful emancipation was to make an annual Thanksgiving Day collection in the forty thousand churches in the United States.

> If the sum averages but *five dollars* per congregation, the aggregate would be *two thousand dollars!* And if this mode is found productive, as it surely would be, the sum raised could be annually increased, the slave holding states and the general government would after a time, lend their cooperation; till, finally, every obstacle to the *real freedom* of America would be melted before the gushing streams of sympathy and charity, as the ice of the polar snow fields yields to the warm rains of summer.

The sums realized could then be used to buy the freedom of the slaves and pay their passage to Liberia. This system would be far superior to total emancipation which was bound to be as disastrous for the freed slaves as for the economy of the South.

In the preface to the revised 1852 edition of *Northwood*, Sarah explained her reasons for reprinting the novel at that particular time and gave her views on the complex problem of slavery.

> Men and women are seeking for light to guide them in the way of duty. That it is easier to burn a temple than to build one, and that two wrongs never make one right, are points conceded by all; yet all seem not to have considered what is quite as sure, that fraud and falsehood never promote the cause of goodness, nor can physical force make or keep men free.... The great error of those who would sever the Union rather than see a slave within its borders, is, that they forget that the *master* is their brother, as well as the *servant*; and that the spirit which seeks to do good to all and evil to none is the only true Christian philanthropy.

These identical views were voiced by Lincoln many times before the final rift.

The following year, 1853, Sarah published her novel *Liberia* to stress the importance of education before emancipation. Liberia is pictured as a beautiful country with ideal weather. Sarah said that schools were being erected to provide an education and to teach trades to the colonists. Crops flourished in the virgin soil.

In the novel she gave fictional case histories of slaves, untaught and unskilled, who gained their freedom only to sink to the lowest levels of poverty and degradation in the alien world outside of the plantation. One man was successful in finding work and providing for his family because his enlightened master had insisted on his learning to read and write before being set free.

Sarah the novelist did not hesitate to take a stand on this very controversial issue. Sarah the editor had very little to say in *Godey's,* and for this she was severely criticized. In November of 1829 she spoke out in favor of the Liberian experiment in the *Ladies' Magazine,* but there she was given a free rein in choosing her subjects. It was an entirely different situation as literary editor of the *Book*; the owner made his stand on the matter very clear, insisting that no material of a religious or political nature appear on the pages of *his* magazine. He proved this point in his handling of the "Grace Greenwood" incident. Godey, always the astute businessman, had many "dear readers" in the South and he had no intention of offending them in any way.

Grace Greenwood was the pen name for Sarah Jane Clark Lippincott who wrote light, amusing stories for the *Lady's Book.* Her first contribution appeared in 1846 and her popularity grew so rapidly that Godey gave her an editorial position on his staff in 1849, a move he regretted before the year was over. Mrs. Lippincott sent a pro-abolition article to the *National Era* and the southern press flew into a rage. How could the publisher sanction such an editor? Quickly defending his stand after an attack by the South Carolina *Telegraph*, Godey said, "I have been publishing the *Lady's Book* for twenty years, *and if in that time one line can be found aspersing in any way Southern institutions, I am willing to fall under your censure.*" Then he added, "I send you a January number. *You will see that Grace Greenwood's name is withdrawn from the cover*, where it was placed nominally as editor, she never having had the least control of its columns."

While he was trying to smooth down ruffled feathers in the South, Godey managed to stir up a hornet's nest in the northern press. One writer included Sarah in his attack on the action taken by the *Book*; Charles Cleveland regretted the fact that Sarah did not resign her position when Mrs. Lippincott was fired. She stayed on as literary editor, but she also continued giving favorable reviews of some of the works of "Grace Greenwood" in the magazine.

Sarah was heartsick when war broke out, yet news about the war was noticeably lacking on the pages of the *Lady's Book.* At the end of 1862 when peace seemed no nearer, she explained to "faithful friends" the role she hoped the magazine was playing during the war-torn years. "If the physical world were convulsed with storms, and the elements of nature seemed charged with destructive power, would it not be a blessed relief to find 'a lodge in the wilderness?' An oasis in the desert? A quiet, cultural garden on which the burning lava had not even breathed?" Her aim was to make the magazine just such an oasis.

She added that her prayer for 1863 was "May those dark

shadows be swept away by the brightness of joys which our Father in Heaven has the power to bestow on us in the coming year!" What would the new year bring? If Sarah had possessed the gift to see into the future, she would have been much pleased to know of her fall Thanksgiving Day triumph, but first came the spring and in May she was to suffer a great personal loss, the death of her daughter and namesake.

In 1857 Josepha had opened a school for girls in Philadelphia which was advertised each month in a space following Sarah's editorial in the "Editor's Table." The school was called Miss S. J. Hale's Boarding and Day School. A lead-in line appeared in January 1863: "This school has now started on its seventh year, its success and present prosperity are very satisfactory to its friends." Then in place of the July advertisement was a black-bordered square containing a notice headed *OBITUARY*.

> We have the sorrowful task of recording, here, where the notice of "Miss S. J. Hale's School" has so long appeared, that her duties on earth are closed.
>
> Miss Sarah Josepha Hale died May 3d, suddenly at the last, although her health had been failing for several months; still she had been able to manage the concerns of the school till the last day of her life. Endeared to all who knew her, and greatly beloved by the young hearts she had carefully trained to occupy woman's true place in the world, while earnestly seeking the heavenly inheritance, she was, in the prime of womanhood, taken from the world by her Almighty Father to enjoy the rewards of the redeemed in Heaven. The mourning hearts she left behind feel that her immortal gain is to them an irreparable loss, and thus as mother, sister, teacher, and friend, her loss cannot but be mourned deeply and long.

Josepha was only forty-two years old.

There was little in the 1865 May edition of the *Lady's Book* to indicate that the war had finally come to an end except for Louis Godey's boyish enthusiasm which bubbled over with the news that mail service was resumed between the North and the South. He wrote "Thanks! Thanks! to our southern Subscribers—Our increase has been greatly beyond our fondest expectations." And this in spite of an increase in the price of the periodical.

Godey's "Arm-Chair" chat the following month took on a somber tone. "We Mourn! Our Chief has Fallen! ABRAHAM LINCOLN IS DEAD!" The obituary notice said "Go where you will—through our principal streets, our courts, our alleys—you will discover a general mourning. It seems not only a mourning for the President of the United States, but a mourning for the just and good man, ABRAHAM LINCOLN." In a longer July editorial the publisher wrote about Lincoln's kindliness with people, all sorts of people. "Never, perhaps, has there been a Ruler so endeared personally to the people, whose welfare he guided, as Abraham Lincoln. He was emphatically the *beloved* of the people."

The first mention Sarah made of the war's end came in her November editorial which combined Thanksgiving Day with peace, brotherhood, and Union. After the quote from St. Luke's account of the Christmas story, "Glory to God in the highest, on earth peace, good-will toward men," she wrote, "Never, since the night when the angels shouted their glad tidings of great joy over Judea, has any nation on earth had such a glorious opportunity of echoing back to Heaven this song of joy and thanksgiving, for the blessings of peace and good-will, as the American people have now before them."

The editorial traced the progress of the establishment of a national Thanksgiving Day, including her long effort in the cause. Then she said that when Lincoln answered her appeal by his Thanksgiving Proclamation in 1863,

> he was not able to influence the States in rebellion, so that festival was, necessarily, incomplete. President Johnson has a happier lot. His voice will reach all American citizens. From East to West, from North to South, the whole country will be moved at his bidding; at home or abroad, on sea or land, the appointed day will be welcomed as the seal of national peace.... [Then on Thanksgiving Day] all our people, as one Brotherhood, will rejoice together, and give thanks to God for our National, State, and family blessings.

18 Woman's Sphere

Ralph Nading Hill wrote:

> Sarah Hale seems, at first blush, to have been a perfect
> contradiction, not only in her looks and actions but in
> what she said and did. A wholesome, soft-spoken mother
> of five children, she was the antithesis of the seriocomic
> suffragette. With a clear conscience Mrs. Hale could an-
> nounce that "the most important vocation on earth is that
> of the Christian mother in her nursery," and at the same
> time be leading campaigns for women doctors, nurses,
> professors, missionaries, sales clerks, and waiters. The edi-
> tor of a magazine for elegant women, she could decry the
> wasp waist and drive her readers out of their parlors into
> the sunshine (but not—Heaven forbid!—in bloomers).

Sarah was not a suffragette, either seriocomic or otherwise,
and she stated her message loud and clear. *Let women be women
and men be men!* Why should women wear "bloomers" and im-
itate the male sex when they have their own sphere of influence,
one in which they are preeminent? And yes, the home is the ideal
place for women to exert their influence (but not—Heaven
forbid!—in the ballot box).

It is easy today to wag an accusing finger at Sarah for her
stand against woman suffrage, and yet her position was not taken
from weakness; she was never afraid to swim against the tide of

public opinion. She sincerely believed with many of her contemporaries, that the great agitation astir in 1869 to gain the vote for women would result in "discord and failure" and be a threat to the security and sanctity of the home, a step which, in her opinion, should be avoided at all costs. But this was not the denial of a right. Women were granted the *privilege* of not being thrust into the political arena. No woman in her era was more pro-woman than Sarah; none worked more tirelessly for the "rights" of her sex. Her great interest in woman's economic independence can be seen by a random selection of progress reports on her editorial pages.

May 1847. "RIGHTS OF MARRIED WOMEN — A Savings' Bank is to be established at Newark, N. J., including the provision that any married woman may in her own name deposit money earned by her own labor or received from others than her husband, the deposits and increases to be payable to her free from the claim of her husband or his creditor."

August 1853. "WOMAN'S RIGHT. — INDORSING NOTES. — The Governor of Missouri, in his message, made one admirable suggestion, that *no man shall be allowed to indorse another man's notes without the consent of the indorser's wife,* or rather, that no indorsement without such consent shall be valid."

Then, on the same editorial page, was another notice of further progress under the heading "PENNSYLVANIA FOR WOMEN. — This noble old State is now taking the lead in the movement so important to the real progress of humanity. Here the right of married women to hold property is liberally secured; the first Female Medical College has been chartered with powers and rights as ample as those now given to male institutions —." A supreme court decision in September of 1859 gave Michigan women the right "to control in all respects all property acquired" either before or after marriage. How much Sarah had wanted this freedom for the sailors' wives when she was living in Boston!

Along with these progress plugs over the years were articles dealing with job opportunities for women. Was this a contradiction to her statement about "the most important vocation on earth"? Sarah was not trying to draw women out of the home, but she sought more options for those who were forced to work. She recommended the position of postmistress for "widows and single women." In 1862 she discovered that only four hundred post offices out of the forty thousand in the nation were run by women. "Before the year closes, we hope there will be at least *four thousand* postmistresses commissioned; and if women, who need the office and can command the requisite credentials, would at once make application, we cannot believe they would be refused."

Sarah's modern approach to many of women's problems did not extend to matters of propriety; she was very much the proper Victorian when it came to women making a display of themselves in public. She and her friend Elizabeth Oakes Smith had a falling out over this question of propriety. Elizabeth was the first woman in the country to tour, from 1851 to 1857, the lyceum circuit as a lecturer. She was a writer, social reformer, and staunch advocate of woman's rights, but not a radical. Many years later she wrote in her "Journal" about the break-up of their friendship.

> Mrs. Hale, like Catherine Beecher and many others, believed it an indecorous thing for a woman to speak in public. To mount the rostrum and give utterance to her own views or opinions was presumptuous, if not to say indecent. We had been friends for many years, and though, as my mentor, she not infrequently took me to task for tendencies of thought not in accord with her own views, she still did not abate her warm affection for me. But when I appeared in the lecture-room, the first woman that ever lectured before the lyceums of the country, she wrote me a severe letter of condemnation; and when I was invited to lecture in Philadelphia ... my old friend refused to hear me or call on me.
>
> This was a painful experience and I took it to heart rather seriously, but the noble Lucretia Mott comforted me with her common-sense view of the matter. Mrs. Hale, said Lucretia, "in theory believed in the entire subordination of women to the other sex; but her practice was somewhat the reverse, and no one acted more independently than she."

In one breath Sarah is criticized for placing woman on a pedestal and in the next for her belief in "the entire subordination of women to the other sex," two views difficult to reconcile. Her writings and action disprove both statements. She did place man firmly at the head of the household, but his wife stood by his side, a companion and helpmate, as they worked out family problems together. There should definitely be no double standard in marriage. "Although all masculine writers hold the opinion that women were made to be married, they do not agree that all men were meant to be married. They believe, too, that woman's noblest virtues of conduct are called forth, and her highest excellence of character perfected, in domestic life; in short, that her destiny is marriage, and her place of honor and happiness is her home." But do they say the same for men? "Yet, if marriage is the best state for women, it should be the best for man; or the plan of creation would seem to be at fault. 'Be ye not unequally yoked' was the great apostle's command to Christians; if men are losers by the union, then marriage is 'unequal' for men."

Another point Sarah stressed was that boys should be taught lessons of tenderness and respect for women. Girls are trained to become good wives and devoted mothers. "Is this lesson of making good husbands and fathers pressed on the mind of boys, or even hinted at in college-classes for young men?"

In a happy home the wife always places her husband's happiness first and he hers. Then with God's help the home will be "happy in love and radiant with the honor which entire goodness and true faithfulness in all relations of life require."

The wife was never meant to be a household drudge. Every labor and time-saving invention to benefit the housewife had Sarah's enthusiastic backing, from "a double skillet for boiling milk" and a "particularly useful rotary egg-beater" to washing and sewing machines. In January 1853 Sarah asked inventors of the country to put their heads together and come up with a machine for washing clothes. "If any can set their wits to work and contrive a suitable apparatus, we will undertake to publish an account of it."

A year and a half later a strange looking, barrel-shaped machine turned by cogwheels and a lever appeared in the *Book* with a rave by Sarah. "For ourselves our spirits fall with the rising steam in the kitchen, and only return to normal temperature when the clothes are folded in the ironing basket. We rejoice that a better day is at hand, and consider the invention described below as full of deepest interest to our sex as housekeepers...."

Then in July of 1860 her enthusiasm for the new sewing machine spilled from one full page over onto the next. "By this invention the needlewoman is enabled to perform her labors in comfort; tasks that used to require the midnight watches by the pale light of a single lamp, and drag through, perhaps, twenty hours, she can now complete in two or three hours. She is thus able to rest at night and have time through the day for family occupations and enjoyments. Is not this a great gain for the good?"

Knowing that many women would not be able to afford to buy a sewing machine, Sarah made an excellent suggestion. Why not form neighborhood clubs, buy a machine together, and then "the long seams, the never ending hems, the hard sewing are all done as by fairy fingers." Her idea took hold and spread rapidly. Sarah mentioned some of the clubs that had been started at the same time as she encouraged other women to follow their good example.

No discussion of woman's rights and privileges would be complete without the most important one of all, the right to equal educational opportunities. One writer stated that Sarah did not object to the word "obey" in the marriage ceremony as long as women could *read* the word. Over fifty percent of women in her time were illiterate. More education would, in addition to making better wives and mothers, make better housekeepers. In her book *Manners* Sarah pointed out that "the more knowledge a woman possesses of the great principles of morals, philosophy and human happiness, the more importance she will attach to her station, and to the name of 'a good housekeeper.'"

In a brief history of "Periodical Literature" appearing in the January "Editors' Table" in 1869, Sarah quoted from her own *Ladies' Magazine* of 1829 to show "the scope of changes advocated for woman's improvement in education and usefulness, and the principles on which we found the progress of feminine influence for the benefit of humanity." Her goal then had been "to arouse her sex in the consideration of the vast power God has given them over the human mind, by committing the infancy of men as well as women entirely to their care. Women, therefore, are in fact the tutors of men, and the sentiments of a man may well be appropriately quoted to show the extent of feminine influence in his early years." Next in rank of importance in moral influence is the *schoolmaster*, and Sarah's second aim had been "to unite the perfection of these two characters, that of excellent mothers and excellent instructresses, with the name of *woman*."

Sarah was pleased and proud to report the great progress that had been made during her forty years as an editor. "There are now in the United States over *one hundred thousand* young women thus employed in the Public Schools, and they are taking the place of men more and more every year. In Boston nine-tenths of the public school teachers are women."

"Thus a learned profession has been opened for women, such as the world has never before offered. To qualify themselves to sustain this great honor and trust worthily is now one of the most important problems of the day." Another challenge. The fact that Sarah was over eighty did not deter her from beginning another drive to advance the educational opportunities for women.

> We need Free National Normal Schools to fit young women for their office of teachers. Congress should be requested to aid. An appeal will be probably made at this session. While wishing our readers a Happy New Year, and offering them this new volume of the *Lady's Book*, we must express our hope that they, and all the women of the United States, will join us in asking aid to found Free National Normal Schools for the daughters of America.

19   One Woman's Record

In January of 1869 Louis Godey had his own New Year's message at the beginning of his "Arm-Chair"department. "A Happy New Year to all! We are truly grateful that we have been spared another year to send forth to our 500,000 readers this annual greeting." Then Mr. Godey, far from the most modest of individuals, used several columns to elaborate on his favorite subject—the wonderful reception his *Book* was still being given, the reasons for its continued popularity, and all the wonderful features to expect in the coming year. "We have little space to spare to write our own commendations. Our continued large list of subscribers best speak for us. A work published for nearly thirty-nine years, and at all times maintaining its proud superiority, is the best recommendation. Had we the room and the inclination, we could fill pages with the kind commendatory letters we receive." Before reaching the end of his "Arm-Chair" chat, the genial editor could not resist publishing a "handsome compliment to our Mrs. Hale from the *Dallas* (Texas) *Herald*."

After a brief comment about the excellence of the *Lady's Book* and its superb publisher, the Herald editor wrote

> And Mrs. Hale—here is a name known wherever literature and social worth are admitted. The time beyond which we knew her not is a dim dream of the past. Her charming stories, well-informed, elegantly-written essays, and sweet, natural poems won the heart of the child, the admiration

of the youth, and the high respect and sincere gratitude of the man. Full of years and full of honors, she holds a place in the esteem of every intelligent and true hearted American.

These complimentary words were followed by a flowery, typically Victorian description of Sarah's appearance and ability which ended with the eulogy, "The Greeks inscribed the names of Lord Byron, Daniel Webster, Henry Clay, and other illustrious friends of Greece upon the peribolus of their Senate chamber. There is a name inscribed high upon the pillars of the world, of which every American can be proud—That name is SARAH JOSEPHA HALE."

This glowing compliment from a fellow editor must have pleased Sarah, but she was far too busy in the present to be concerned with future laurels. One very time-consuming project was the researching and editing of her most prodigious literary work, *Woman's Record, or Sketches of Distinguished Women*. The first printing in 1853 was followed by two revised editions, the last in 1876. The final edition was made up of thirty-six volumes with 230 portraits "Engraved in Wood by Lossing and Barritt."

This ambitious project traced the influence of women, through their writing, on social organizations and literature from "The Beginning" through 1868. It was divided into four eras: the first period before the birth of Christ, the second up to 1500, the third 1500 to 1800, and the final one almost two-thirds of the nineteenth century. In the "Introduction" to this last period, Sarah was happy and proud to report that

> each year brings the public mind more into harmony with the views advanced, namely, — that on the right influence of women depends the moral improvement of men; and that the condition of the female sex decides the destiny of the nation. American Legislators are awakening to these truths; within the last fifteen years, laws more equitable in regard to property rights of married women have been enacted; the education of girls is more liberally provided for; Colleges and "Schools of Design for Women" have been incorporated; Medical Science is open to women;

their future as physicians for their own sex admitted; and over three hundred women have received the full diploma of M. D. As teachers, young women are taking the place of men everywhere in our public schools, to the acknowledged improvement of national education.

During the present century, these ideas of the true mission of women have been developed. Within the last fifty years more books have been written by and about women than all put forth in the preceeding five thousand eight hundred years of the world. ...Women write the majority of children's books, and of religious and Sunday School books in general. They contribute largely to periodical literature.

In other fields great changes were also taking place. The number of proficient women painters was increasing rapidly and there was even "a sculptress of note—Miss Ida Waugh." Women missionaries were active in India, Africa, Turkey, Brazil, and New Mexico; and thanks to Sarah, quite a few were medical missionaries though the author took no credit for this contribution.

The amount of research required for the *Woman's Record* was staggering. Over two thousand women were given recognition in varying degrees of detail depending on material sources and Sarah's opinion of their importance. Her judgment in most instances was very sound except when it came to evaluating poetry. So much verse that was extremely popular in the nineteenth century has not stood the test of time, which is true of her own poetry, and yet in the autobiographical section of her *Record*, she gave no prose selections, only poetry. When the final edition of *Woman's Record* was published in 1876, Sarah was eighty-eight years old and still active as an editor.

At the time Sarah had turned seventy-five, she had, as a concession to age, changed her work routine; except for occasional visits, she no longer went to the publishing house. Her new office was her large airy room on the second floor in the home of her daughter Frances and her doctor-husband. Her grandson Richard Hunter acted as her go-between. He did the footwork and helped with some of the office chores, a most convenient and pleasant arrangement.

The room could not have been better suited to her tastes. It stretched across the entire front of the house with windows overlooking the tree-shaded street. An alcove almost hid her bed and bureau, leaving the rest of the area for her living-room office with its focal point the huge table desk in the center of the room. Larger even than her keeping room in Newport, it had the same warm charm and look of comfort. A long sofa was placed in front of one of the windows; but instead of two armchairs before a fireplace, there was one favorite rocker that in cool weather could be pulled up by the open hearth of a Franklin stove. Books, books, and more books. Ceiling-to-floor shelves around the room were broken only by the doors and windows, and these bookcases were filled to capacity.

The room was rarely completely silent because of four pairs of canaries suspended in four cages near the windows, a captured rememberance of the bird songs she had loved so dearly as a girl in Newport. Another tangible link with the past was the ever-present bowl of grapes on her desk. Scores of people were drawn to this pleasant oasis. Long after her grandson Richard Hunter had acted as her righthand helper, he spoke of his grandmother's magnetic charm and warm personality. "I remember streams of people going upstairs to grandmother's room. Everybody who came to Philadelphia must have called on her, and of course there were always her many local friends and the endless authors and artists who contributed to the magazine."

In 1876 when Philadelphia spread out her red carpet to welcome visitors to the city's celebration of our country's important birthday party, Sarah sent a message to her home town inviting all who came for the centennial to drop in to see her. Many Newporters were delighted to have the chance to talk with their most famous native, and Sarah made them feel welcomed.

In December of that year Louis Godey was negotiating the sale of his magazine and his chat with his readers reflected the coming change.

> This number will close the ninety-third volume of the *Lady's Book*—558 monthly numbers! Forty-six years and six months of editorial labor! During all those years there has never been a failure or delay. We feel proud of its age, we feel proud of its success, we feel proud of its prospects

for continued prosperity, and today, as we send forth the
last editorial of this centennial year, we feel that, with the
union we have formed with the younger branch of our
establishment, the hopes and wishes of many of our ex-
changes will be fully realized.

The following year when the final papers were passed, Godey
retired from his long partnership with his beloved *Book*, a retire-
ment that lasted only a few months. He did not live to see a
gradual decline of the magazine under the management of the new
owner, Frank A. Munsey.

Sarah wrote her last editorial in December of 1877 just before
Munsey took over. Her message was addressed to the women of
America and she expressed her hopes for the future more person-
ally by dropping the editorial "we." At the end she said

And now, having reached my ninetieth year, I must bid
farewell to my countrywomen, with the hope that this
work of half a century may be blessed to the furtherance of
their happiness and usefulness in their Divinely appointed
sphere. New avenues for higher culture and for good
works are opening before them, which fifty years ago were
unknown. That they may improve these opportunities,
and be faithful to their high vocation, is my heartfelt
prayer.

Sarah did not put down her pen at the end of her editorial
career; for the remaining sixteen months of her life, she continued
her long practice of writing letters—many letters. A compliment
she received in a personal thank-you note for the gift of one of her
autographed books must have made her feel justly proud. President Hayes wrote that the book she sent was "prized especially as
the gift of a lady who has accomplished so much for the peace and
happiness of the American people as yourself."

At the halfway mark of her ninety-first year, Sarah died
peacefully on April 30, 1879. Her funeral was attended by hundreds. One old friend wrote her a compliment that sums up the
measure of her life's work. Oliver Wendell Holmes said, "How
much you have done, and always with a high and pure aim!"

Bibliography

Short quotations have been taken from the works marked with an asterisk(*).

Bacon, Edwin, *Boston Illustrated,* 1872; Revised edition 1890.

Baldorff, V.R. "Thanksgiving, a Woman's Gift to the Nation." *Independent Woman* 33 (November 1954):403.

Bishop, H.O. "Thanksgiving Day's Origin." *National Republic* 18 (November 1930):8.

Bowen, Catherine Drinker. *Yankee from Olympus.* Boston: Little Brown & Co., 1944.

Brown, Herbert Ross. *The Sentimental Novel in America, 1789-1860.* Durham, NC: Duke University Press, 1940.

Buell, Jonathan S. *Record of the Buell Family.* Volume 3. 1881.

Burt, Olive (Wooley). "First Woman Editor." *Hobbies* 59 (August 1954): 77.

Charlton, Edwin A. *New Hampshire As It Is.* Claremont, NH: Tracy and Sanford, 1855.

Cheney, G.A. "Newport Today—Its Men and Affairs." *Granite Monthly* 40 (August 1908): 263-4.

Crawford, Mary Caroline. *Romantic Days and Ways of Old Boston.* Boston, 1910.

Dougherty, A.W. "Mother of Thanksgiving." *Overland* 86 (November 1928): 381.

Drake, Samuel Adams. *Old Landmarks and Historic Personages of Boston.* Boston: Roberts Brothers, 1883.

Edes, Samuel and Edes, Marcia J., comp. *The Book of Old Newport.* Newport, NH: Press of the Argus and Spectator, 1909.

*Entrikin, Isabell Webb. *Sarah Josepha Hale and Godey's Lady's Book.* Lancaster, PA: Lancaster Press, Inc., 1946.

Farwell, Mary. *Early Days on the Boston Common.* n.d.

*Finley, Ruth E. *The Lady of Godey's: Sarah Josepha Hale.* Philadelphia: J.R. Lippincott, 1931.

Forbes, Frank H. *Days and Ways of Old Boston.* Edited by William Rossiter. 1915.

Gilman, Arthur. *The Story of Boston.* New York: G.P.Putnam Sons, 1889.

Griffith, George Bancroft. "The Author of 'Mary's Little Lamb.' " *Granite State Magazine* 1 (May 1906): 210-14.

*Haight, Elizabeth Hazelton, ed. *The Autobiography and Letters of Matthew Vassar.* New York: Oxford University Press, 1916.

Haight, Gordon A. *Mrs. Sigourney, The Sweet Singer of Hartford.* New Haven: Yale University Press, 1930.

Hale, Richard Walden. "Mary Had a Little Lamb, and Its Author." *Century Magazine* 67 (March 1904): 738-42.

Hale, R. W. "Mrs. Sarah Josepha Hale." *Century Magazine* 45: 738.

Hale, Robert Safford. *Genealogy of the Descendants of Thomas Hale, of Wallon, England and Newbury, Massachusetts.* Albany, NY: Weed, 1889.

Hammond, Otis G. *Checklist of New Hampshire Local History.* Concord, NH: New Hampshire Historical Society, 1925.

Hart, John S. *Female Prose Writers of America.* Philadelphia: Butler, 1852.

*Hill, Ralph Nading. "Mr. Godey's Lady." *American Heritage* 9 (October 1958):20-27.

Holmes, Oliver Wendell. *Autocrat at the Breakfast Table.* 1882.

Howe, M.A. DeWolfe. *Boston, The Place and the People.* New York: Hastings House, 1946.

Jackson, Joseph. *Literary Landmarks of Philadelphia.* Philadelphia: McKay, 1939.

Johnson, Gerald W. *Mount Vernon, The Story of a Shrine.* New York: Random House, 1953.

Kirker, Harold and Kirker, James. *Bulfinch's Boston, 1787-1817.* 1964.

*King, Grace Elizabeth. *Mount Vernon on the Potomac.* History of the Mount Vernon's Ladies' Association of the Union, 1929.

"The Lady Editor Who Paid Poe Fifty Cents Per Page." *Current Opinion* 62 (March 1917): 204.

*Lutz, Alma. *Emma Willard, Daughter of Democracy.* Boston: Houghton, 1929.

*Martin, Lawrence. "The Genesis of Godey's Lady's Book." *New England Quarterly* I (January 1928).

Metcalf, Henry H. "Newport: A Model New England Town." *Granite Monthly* 20 (January 1896):1-31.

Morris, Charles. *Makers of Philadelphia.* Philadelphia: Hamersly, 1894.

Mott, Frank Luther. *A History of American Magazines, 1741-1850.* Cambridge: Harvard University Press, 1939.

Nash, Elizabeth Todd. *Fifty Puritan Ancestors, 1628-1660*. New Haven: Tuttle, 1902.

"Newport's 150th Anniversary." *Granite Monthly* 43 (August/September 1911):232-75.

Oberholtzer, Ellis P. *The Literary Landmarks of Philadelphia*. Philadelphia: Jacobs, 1906.

*Packard, Alpheus S. "History of the Bunker Hill Monument." *Maine Historical Society Collections*, III (1853):241-69.

*Parmelee, Joseph W. "History of Newport" in *History of Cheshire and Sullivan Counties*, edited by D. Hamilton Hurd. Philadelphia: J.W.Lewis & Co., 1886.

Pattee, Fred Lewis. *The Feminine Fifties*. New York: Appleton, 1940.

Read, Thomas Buchanan, *The Female Poets of America*. 4th ed. Philadelphia: Butler, 1851.

Ross, Marjorie Drake. *The Book of Boston*. 1961

*Rossiter, William, ed. *Days and Ways of Old Boston*. 2d edition. Boston: R.H.Sterns & Co., 1914.

*Sanford, Lucy E. "Mrs. Sarah J. Hale." *Granite Monthly* 3 (March 1880): 208-11.

Savage, James. *Genealogical Dictionary of the First Settlers of New England*. 1860.

Stowe, Harriet Beecher. *Uncle Tom's Cabin*. 1852.

Tarbell, I.M. "Editor of Godey's Lady's Book." *American Magazine* 69 (March 1910): 666-68.

Taylor, William R. *Cavalier and Yankee, The Old South & American National Character*. Cambridge, Mass.: Harvard University Press, 1979.

"The True Story of Mary's Little Lamb." *The Dearborn Independent* 27 (March 26, 1927): 12-13,20-22.

Tyron, W.S. *Parnassus Corner, A Life of James T. Fields*. 1963.

Trollope, Frances. *Domestic Manners of the Americans*. New York: Dodd, 1832-1927.

Warner, Richard Fay. "Godey's Lady's Book." *American Mercury* 2 (August 1924): 399-402.

Watkins, Walter K. *History of Tremont Street and Temple Place*. n.d.

*Wheeler, Edmund. *The History of Newport, N.H., from 1766 to 1878*. Concord, NH: Republican Press Assoc., 1879.

"When Edgar Allan Poe Wrote for Fifty Cents a Page." *New York Times* 66 (January 28, 1917):section 5, p.14.

*Wyman, Mary Alice, Ed. Transcript of *The Autobiography of Elizabeth Oakes Smith*. Portland, Maine: Maine Historical Society Library, 1924.

Periodicals edited by Sarah Josepha Hale:

*The Ladies' Magazine. Boston: Putnam and Hunt, 1828-1830. Vols. 1-3
                    Boston: Marsh, Capen and Lyon, 1831. Vol. 4
*The Ladies' Magazine and Literary Gazette. Boston: Marsh, Capen &
          Lyon, 1832-1833. Vols. 5-6.
*The American Ladies' Magazine. Boston: James B. Dow, 1834-1836.
          Vols. 7-9.
*Godey's Lady's Book. Philadelphia: Godey, January 1837-December
          1877. Vols. 14-95.

*The following books, written by Sarah Josepha Hale, were used in the
preparation of this work.*

Flora's Interpreter; or, The American Book of Flowers and Sentiments.
          Boston, Marsh, Capen & Lyon, 1832.
The Genius of Oblivion; and other Original Poems. By a lady of New
          Hampshire. Concord: Jacob B. Moore, 1823.
Harry Guy, the Widow's Son. A Story of the Sea. Boston: B.B. Mussey
          and Co., 1848.
Ladies' New Book of Cookery: A Practical System. New York: H. Long
          & Brother, 1852.
The Ladies' Wreath; a Selection from the Female Poetic Writers of Eng-
          land and America. Marsh, Capen & Lyon, 1837.
Keeping House and House Keeping. New York: Harper & Brothers, 1845.
Love; or, Woman's Destiny, a Poem. Philadelphia: Duffield Ashmead, 1870.
Manners; or Happy Homes and Good Society all the Year Round. Bos-
          ton: J.E. Tilton and Co., 1867.
The Monument. Boston (107: Sept. 8-15, 1840).
Northwood; or Life North & South. 2nd edition.
          New York: H. Long & Parather, 1852.
Poems for Our Children. Boston: Marsh, Capen & Lyon, 1830.
Traits of American Life. Philadelphia: E.L.Carey and A. Hart, 1835.
Woman's Record: or, Sketches of All Distinguished Women. New
          York: Harper & Brothers, 1853.

Index